Revelation

by Robert H. Conn

General Editor, Lynne M. Deming
Assistant Editor, Margaret Rogers
Copy Processing, Sylvia Marlow
Cover Design by Harriet Bateman

ISBN 0-939697-37-8

Table of Contents

Outline of Revelation

I. The Prologue (1:1-8)
   A. The source of John's message (1:1-3)
   B. Greetings to the seven churches (1:4-8)

II. John's Call to Prophesy (1:9-20)
   A. The call and the command (1:9-11)
   B. The *one like a son of man* (1:12-16)
   C. An order and an explanation (1:17-20)

III. Letters to Three Churches (2:1-17)
   A. The letter to Ephesus (2:1-7)
   B. The letter to Smyrna (2:8-11)
   C. The letter to Pergamum (2:12-17)

IV. Letters to Four Churches (2:18–3:22)
   A. The letter to Thyatira (2:18-29)
   B. The letter to Sardis (3:1-6)
   C. The letter to Philadelphia (3:7-13)
   D. The letter to Loadicea (3:14-22)

V. The Vision From Heaven (4:1–5:14)
   A. The heavenly praise of God (4:1-11)
   B. The scroll and the Lamb (5:1-14)

VI. The Seven Seals (6:1–8:5)
   A. The first four seals (6:1-8)
   B. The fifth and sixth seals (6:9-17)
   C. God's people on earth and in heaven (7:1-17)
   D. The seventh seal (8:1-5)

VII. The Seven Trumpets (8:6–11:19)
   A. The first four trumpets (8:6-13)
   B. The sixth and seventh trumpets (9:1-21)
   C. The small scroll (10:1-11)
   D. The two martyrs (11:1-14)
   E. The seventh trumpet (11:15-19)

VIII. A Parable About Evil and the Church (12:1–14:20)
   A. The dragon and the woman (12:1-6)
   B. Satan is cast out of heaven (12:7-12)
   C. The dragon pursues the woman (12:13-17)
   D. The dragon's servant: the beast (13:1-10)
   E. A second beast worships the first (13:11-18)
   F. The martyrs worship in heaven (14:1-7)
   G. The fate of the unfaithful (14:8-13)
   H. Judgments begin (14:14-20)

IX. The Seven Bowls of Wrath (15:1–16:21)
   A. The song of the conquerors (15:1-4)
   B. Presentation of the bowls of wrath (15:5-8)
   C. Four bowls of natural disaster (16:1-9)
   D. Three bowls of warfare (16:10-21)

X. The Last Days of Babylon (17:1–18:24)
   A. The harlot and the beast (17:1-6)
   B. The harlot and beast explained (17:7-14)
   C. The fate of the harlot (17:15-18)
   D. The lament of heaven (18:1-8)
   E. The lament of earth (18:9-19)
   F. The angel with a stone (18:20-24)

XI. The Vindication of God (19:1-21)
   A. Voices rise from heaven (19:1-5)
   B. The marriage supper of the Lamb (19:6-10)
   C. The great battle (19:11-21)

Introduction to Revelation

Nearly three hundred miles north of Jerusalem, along the coastline of the Mediterranean, the land juts sharply to the west on what appears on the map to be an enormous peninsula. The coastline, as it bends west, forms the south edge of modern Turkey—land referred to by geographers as Asia Minor. The coast continues unevenly for nearly three hundred miles before it turns north again.

There, at the northward turn, several islands cluster in the Mediterranean. One of them, thirty miles out, is Patmos—in first-century Rome a prison island. Rome used Patmos to isolate political prisoners. Sometime between A.D. 81 and 91 a Christian prophet named John was exiled on Patmos. And, while imprisoned on Patmos, John received the inspiration to write the book we know as Revelation.

We know little about John other than what can be deduced from his writing. We know he wrote during a time when the church was young and faced persecution. He clearly had the care and welfare of the church at heart. And he saw, equally as clearly, the peril faced by the church—partly from persecution and partly from a more subtle danger: affluence. And clearest of all, he had searched the Old Testament (the Bible of the early church) for a key to understanding his times. What was clear to his eyes soon crystalized in his mind, preparing him for the visions he was to see and for the immense task of interpreting and explaining them to the church.

The Historical Setting of Revelation

(1) Rome

From the time of Caesar Augustus, the first Roman emperor (27 B.C.–A.D. 14), to Domitian (A.D. 81-96), the Roman empire reached enormous proportions. It included land from Israel in the south to modern-day England in the north. That expansion took eleven emperors slightly more than 125 years.

Although the Romans tended to rule with an even hand, much depended upon the emotional stability of the emperor. Two, especially, stand out for their instability and violence: Nero (A.D. 54-68) and Domitian. Nero was notoriously vicious and was the first great persecutor of the church. Early tradition accuses him of the deaths of Paul and Peter. The disastrous fire of Rome occurred during his reign and, to counter a pervasive rumor that he had started it, Nero blamed the Christians. Horrible tortures followed. Although the persecutions took place mostly in Rome, word spread and Christians were badly shaken.

Domitian, coming to the throne thirteen years after Nero's death, resumed the violence. Some forms of country- and emperor-worship had accompanied the growth of the empire, but it had never been a life or death issue. Domitian took it seriously. One of the main centers of his cult was the city of Smyrna, and we will see in the Book of Revelation (2:8-11) that Christians in that place faced a very difficult time.

During the time when Revelation was written, Rome had accompanied its vast political expansion with an equally expansive program of business and economics. As John makes vivid in the later chapters of Revelation, Rome kept a world full of nations, builders, craft guilds, bankers, and merchants well occupied. Shipping routes spread from Rome in every direction, tying most of the ancient world to its web. From that rich commerce and its exciting variety of goods and opportunities, Christians found an endless supply of subtle enticements.

(2) The Church

By the time of Domitian, several decisive events had occurred in the church. For one, the Christians who had remained in Jerusalem after Jesus' death had finally left. Within a year after their leaving (A.D. 70), the Jews rebelled against Rome. In retaliation, the Roman army destroyed Jerusalem. From that time on, the early church was cut off from the city of its origin. However, thanks to its kinship with the Jews, it would continue to suffer the aftershocks of persecution aimed at the Jews.

Since Paul's journeys to Asia Minor, that area had responded increasingly well to Christian missionary activity. By A.D. 75, Asia Minor was no longer the mission field, it was the home of the church. The church's roots held more firmly in Asia Minor than anywhere else in the world. Ephesus was its spiritual center, much as Jerusalem had been for the early Christians and for the Jews before them.

The new home was a mixed blessing. Large cities and good ports put the church at the heart of the ancient world. The mission advanced. But advancement brought increased visibility, and when Christians refused to worship the emperor it was even more necessary to make an example of them.

The success of the Christian cause also meant the entry of many Christians into the mainline culture. The subtle temptations of affluence and influence followed. Indeed, John worried as much about that as he did about persecution.

Within the space of two generations, the church had changed its environment from Israel to Asia Minor, had survived the death of nearly all of its founders, and had gone from the exhilaration of rapid expansion to the ravages of unwarranted persecution and the incursion of greed and temptation. By the time John was on Patmos, the worst sides of all of those changes enclosed upon the church. To John, things seemed out of control.

John wrote his book to a church that needed to have its apparent chaos put in the larger perspective of God's controlling purposes. Behind the scenes, he wrote, God is even now making the powers of evil accomplish the divine will. History is coming to its end, but it is the end that God has in mind for it. To the Christians who have given in to temptation, John wrote, "Keep the faith. God knows your sins." To those who kept the faith and suffered the consequences, John wrote, "God is in control. Hold on. Endure!"

(3) The Church Between Two Cultures

During the first century of the Christian church, two great cultures still shaped the thought and life of the people of Asia Minor. Obviously Rome exerted influence. But the area had been dominated by Greece for years before that. Without the resources of mass media, it was not easy for one conquering nation to obliterate the influence of another. It took a great deal of time for the culture of one to replace the other.

For a long time, in Asia Minor, the Greek and Roman cultures coexisted, somewhat like two waves—the first on the shore saturating the sands and then receding, the second overarching and overreaching the first. For a while, although they moved in contrary motion, the two pressed upon the shore simultaneously.

Greek life, lore, and language, first on the shores of Asia Minor, had spread far and soaked deep. The second wave, Rome, rose higher and reached farther, and fell with more oppressive weight.

The Jews had settled in Asia Minor before the time of Jesus, well during the time of Greek control. They spoke Greek. The early Christians, like Paul, spoke Greek. The Gospels were written in a Greek dialect of the common people, called *koine*. All of the books of the New Testament were first written in Greek.

The official language of the Roman Empire was Latin. It

was the language of the new, higher, and larger wave. And it settled over Asia Minor from the top down. That is, it was the language of the politicians, of administration, and of business.

Most people conducted their daily lives in Greek. And that language, too, had its various levels. Philosophy, religion, and much social life found their natural voices speaking Greek. It was the tongue of the cultural highbrow. But it was also, in some of its dialects, the tongue of the street.

The Book of Revelation was not highbrow. John wrote in Greek, not Latin; that is, he wrote in the language of the people and not of the powerful. But he also wrote awkwardly, and was often uncertain about the proper tenses of verbs. His was almost the language of everyday life, of the common folk. In its vitality and color, it was very different from the stern administrative prose of Latin—as different as the clamor of enthusiasm in the streets is from the solemn deliberations of a budget committee.

If we can judge from John's book, then, the early Christians lived between two cultures, not at all members of the dominant class. Nor were they, for the most part, warmly identified with the Greeks. They spoke the language of the common person, not the intellectual, and they worked most closely, at least at first, with the Greek- speaking Jews who had settled in Asia Minor many years before Rome became its captor.

(4) The Emperors of Rome

The following list of emperors of Rome contains eleven names. In Revelation many references are made through symbolism to the emperors of Rome. Often they refer to the time of Domitian, who ruled during the era in which John wrote. But the references are confusing. For example, he is, at times, considered the seventh emperor.

At other times, it is assumed that Nero, who died in A.D. 68, will arise from the dead and come back to rule, and he will be the eighth emperor. To further confuse the matter, it may also be the case that Domitian is referred to as though he were a second Nero.

We do not know how John kept count. But most scholars agree that he probably did not regard Galba, Otho, and Vitellius as emperors. They each reigned briefly during a time of great confusion, and met unfortunate deaths. None had much to do with shaping the contours of Roman history.

One suggestion for understanding John's references to the seven emperors is to remember that seven is a number for completeness. He may simply have had in mind the entire leadership of Rome up to his time.

Augustus: 27 B.C.–A.D. 14
Tiberius: A.D. 14-37
Caligula: 37-41
Claudius: 41-54
Nero: 54-68
Galba: 68-69
Otho: 69
Vitellius: 69
Vespasian: 69-79
Titus: 79-81
Domitian: 81-96

(5) Asia Minor and the Mediterranean Sea

From the maps of the Mediterranean, one can understand the great advantage geography had given Rome. Chapter 18 of the Book of Revelation shows us the merchants of the earth, sobbing at the destruction of that enormous city. (In that chapter *Babylon* is John's special code word for Rome.)

But not only do the merchants sob, the shipmasters and seafaring men also cry out in grief. Not that they regret the fate of the Romans as people. They regret the loss of one of their most lucrative markets.

Rome did receive much of its wealth overland. The roads of all of the lands around the Mediterranean had been made safe for travel. Roman soldiers guarded them. It was thanks to the Romans that Paul and Silas took their missionary journeys safe from harm.

Rome had also cleared the sea of pirates. The nations of the Mediterranean could export and import. Lively commerce arose, with Rome at its center. In fact, Rome became the economic safety net for the entire region.

By John's time, the commercial interests of Rome reached as far overseas as India—to which Rome exported linen, coral, and metals, and from which were imported silks, perfumes, and jewels. Rome was also a vigorous importer of slaves. When one recalls that John refers to Christians as *servants* and that the word he used is the ancient word for *slave*, one knows John had firsthand experience with the absolute obedience required of slaves.

Not only Rome, but two of the cities to which John sent his letters were also important coastal cities: Smyrna and Ephesus. Like Rome, they shared the wealth gained from a thriving import-export business. In these Roman cities, the wares of the entire known world created unrivaled opulence, for some. John knew the strategic importance of Rome at the center of that entire network of buying and selling.

The inland cities to which John wrote in Asia Minor were also strategically located. They were, for the most part, gateway cities—opening to important land routes. Thyatira, for example, lay on a great road that connected the Hermus Valley and the trade centers of the East to the city of Pergamum. Laodicea, considerably south of Thyatira, lay on an important road that began at the coastal city of Ephesus and stretched far into Phrygia. Laodicea may have been the doorkeeper of the most traveled trade route to the West in ancient times.

The area that housed the early church everywhere fed

into the Roman overlord of the house. Revelation is not by accident, then, a book about two cities that contest with each other for control of history. The city of Rome, to John's eyes, reached everywhere through and beyond the visible landscape. Only the city of God had hopes of outreaching it.

Who Is John?

The name *John* was not uncommon in Rome, and it was certainly widely used in the church and in its stories: John the Baptist, John the son of Zebedee, John the author of the Gospel, John the writer of the epistles, John the author of Revelation. Were some of them the same person? Some traditions said yes, some said no. Of all of the writings we have by men named John, the Gospel and the first two epistles seem most similar.

Revelation, however, differs greatly from all of the others. It has a different style, different content, and uses a different vocabulary. Most scholars think the writer of Revelation was not the same person who wrote the Gospel.

But who was he? We don't know who, but we can learn a lot about him from his book. For example, he spoke openly about Christ, even in times when Christians felt immense pressure to worship the emperor. He was faithful during times of persecution—so faithful that the authorities arrested him and exiled him on the island of Patmos.

John was deeply aware of the social and political events of the day. He could grasp their general direction and could measure them by his own rule of faith.

He had a pastor's concern for the churches in Asia Minor. Everything he wrote was directed to those tempted and beleaguered congregations, pointing behind the veil of daily events to the God who was working to save them and to bring history to its end.

He knew the Old Testament well, especially the

prophets and the first five books, the Torah. He had pored over those scrolls in search of the key that unlocked the secret of God's work in history. Old Testament images and symbols became the language of his faith, the way he learned to talk about the world and God's will. And he had found particularly important those prophetic writings called *apocalyptic*. Those books used dramatic images, vivid scenery, and extraordinary stories and parables. Expressing itself in each of them is a testimony to God's glory, to the evil of the times, and to God's soon-to-occur intervention in history on behalf of the faithful.

John was first and foremost a Christian prophet. He believed that God had acted to save human beings through Christ. It was through Christ that he saw into the heart of God's purpose, God's plan to form and preserve the church unto the end of time.

Finally, John was well-known and respected by the Christians in Asia Minor. His book, possibly the only one of its kind to come from a Christian, had to be accepted on the authority of his name alone. He was known well enough to know that that would be enough.

Revelation: The Word and the Book

John's book is sometimes called *Revelation* and sometimes *The Apocalypse*. Both words come down to the same thing. *Apocalypse* comes from two words in the Greek, one meaning "to remove" and the other meaning "the cover." In Greek myth, Calypso, the daughter of Atlas, dwelt upon an island where she kept Ulysses captive, much as John was held captive on Patmos. *Calypso* means "the concealer." Something that reveals what has been concealed is apocalyptic (*apo* means "to remove"). Therefore, the name that is given to Revelation and to many other books that promise to reveal God's hidden plan is *apocalypse*.

The word *revelation* also comes from two words, the

first meaning *to undo* and the second meaning *veil*. A revelation is something that removes the veil and lets us see face-to-face.

More than a word, though, *apocalyptic* is also a form of writing, much as mysteries and romances are forms of writing. The Book of Revelation is written in the form of an apocalypse. But what exactly is an apocalyptic book? It is one that has most of these characteristics:

(1) It bears the name of an important person in religious history. Usually the writings claim to have been written several years earlier, to have been hidden until "just the right time in history," and to have surfaced only recently. Apocalyptic books deal with the present events in a highly symbolic way, therefore, as though the long-dead author had foreseen them much earlier.

(2) It takes the form of a report of visions. The visions usually have remarkably vivid and frequently frightening contents. An apocalypse may contain several visions, each repeating emphases of earlier ones, but repeating them in more intense images.

(3) It uses many symbols, especially combinations of numbers (for example, the number seven meant completeness or perfection to the Jews) or animals or strange creatures that have special meanings.

(4) It emphasizes a present crisis in history. History is portrayed as a struggle between good and evil which now rages toward its final battle. The writer believes the end is near, and encourages the reader to remain faithful even though the force of evil seems almost overwhelming. The writer helps the reader to interpret the signs of the times. Properly read, those signs reveal to the faithful that God is in control.

(5) It holds out hope only in God's intervention. History has strayed beyond the limits of humans to redeem it, and has fallen entirely into the province of evil. Rescue comes only from beyond history, only from God.

(6) It makes many allusions to other books, usually

those of prophets or other apocalyptic writers. It can do this because an apocalypse is, from the beginning, a written book—unlike those of Old Testament prophets or those about Jesus, which were first spoken and then later written down by disciples. The author of an apocalypse sits down to write, not with remembered words in his ear, but with books at his elbow. He has had his vision, and he has his reference books to find the words and symbols he needs in order to describe and interpret them. That way he can write in a way that other readers of prophecies and apocalypses can well understand.

Apocalypse, then, is a vast and energetic reinterpretation of current events. It tells the news, but not from the standpoint of the powerful whose daily profits make everything seem well to them. It tells the news from the standpoint of those who see the ravages of the poor and the high price morality pays for profit. It reports: These are not the best of times but the worst, and God is coming soon.

The Book of Revelation has most of those characteristics. Although it does not claim that its author lived in the past or that it lay hidden long and only recently came to light, it does rely upon striking visions. Combinations of numerical and animal symbols appear on every page. Clearly it describes a crisis of great magnitude occurring in history, spiralling it to its end, and soon. It ascribes its authorship to a writer who bears a famous name in the church.

Further, through each vision the writer testifies to God's coming intervention, and to God's presence in the here and now—the evil powers only think they are in control. Allusions to Isaiah, Exodus, Daniel, Ezekiel, Jeremiah, and Zechariah enliven and inform nearly every vision and parable. The book was certainly a written product from the onset; John is often told to write what he sees, and in 1:13 he promises a blessing to those who read the book aloud in church.

The Book of Revelation, then, is an apocalypse. It is also a powerful Christian political tract for its time. The book radically rejected the way the Romans saw history. The Romans, at the height of their power, had confidence in their cause. From John's point of view, the very things that supported Rome were the cause of crisis. Wealth and power make for impressive governmental statistics.

And when cities begin taking pride in their religious devotions to empire and emperor, the good stars may seem to be in their ascendancy.

For John, wealth spelled temptation and short-sighted satisfaction with splendor. And power, usually corrupting in itself, in the hands of evil could call bad good and destroy those who dared to say otherwise. But worse, power and wealth combined to entice Christians who wanted somehow to have both the fruits of luxury and the benefits of discipleship. Many submitted, and distorted the gospel so they could enjoy sexual and social license and yet claim to be Christians.

John could not allow secular wealth and power the sole right to interpret history. He wrote against the nation that surrounded him and against the influence it was having on the church. That Rome had its own religion and, at times, forced all to worship at its shrines, only added evidence to a case that, in John's mind, had already reached its verdict.

His book makes the case and reveals the verdict. The courtroom has been behind the scenes of history; but what was hidden is now revealed. And, as in any true court of law, justice is rendered. That is good news for the faithful and bad news for the unfaithful. That is also the theme of John's book: Revelation.

How to Read the Book of Revelation

After reading any other book in the New Testament, Revelation comes as quite a surprise. Its images, bold pictures, and sometimes strident voice may make a reader feel uneasy. Its message is disturbing. The fact that it is unrelenting in its insistence that we pay attention only makes us more uneasy. Add to that its display of violence and carnage, and it is little wonder that Christians turn away from its pages.

But the book can be read with great profit. Through even its stormiest passages come rays of the hope that lies behind the book. John did not intend simply to frighten his readers. He wanted to strengthen them. The way he wrote would not have been unfamiliar to first-century Christians. But, because we do not know their tradition, we often fail to see what John was up to.

The following eight suggestions may help you bear with John's book until you become at ease with it. When you do, it will become easier to see the vision of the light that drove him to decry the world's darkness.

These eight suggestions are not "keys" to the book. They do not pretend that Revelation is a single large and secret code from which we can decipher each jot and tittle of history. They do offer you a way of identifying several of the things John does. When you begin to see how he works, and to recognize the patterns he uses, you may feel encouraged to venture interpretations of your own.

(1) Realize that Revelation, while it is unique in the New Testament, was not unusual in its time. There had been other books like it, some in the Old Testament, and some elsewhere. While no other New Testament books are completely like it, some parts of those books have sections that are similar to Revelation. The most famous of those is called "The Little Apocalypse" and is found in the Gospel of Mark (see Mark, Chapter 13).

(2) Realize that John did not write in a vacuum. He had a library, and Revelation was written by quoting sources

from several other books in his library. In the commentary section of this book, we will call your attention to many of them. Whatever John's visions were, he turned often to his favorite books to help him describe what he saw and to interpret it to his readers. Among his favorite books were these from the Old Testament: Genesis, Exodus, Psalms, Isaiah, Ezekiel, Jeremiah, and Daniel. As you read Revelation and this commentary, make a note of which parts of those books John relies on the most.

(3) Study the outline of Revelation in this book. Notice the patterns in it. There are several sets of sevens—letters to seven churches, seven seals, seven bowls. The number seven is symbolic is this book. It refers to perfection or to completeness. Thus, the seven churches represent not only themselves, but all of the church.

Look at the progression of the book. View it as a single extended sermon, making one point in several ways, each way more dramatic and powerful than the one before.

Notice that the book ends with what looks like a triumph: The Holy City. Think about other stories you have read in which there are days of hard trial and great jeopardy, stories about difficult journeys leading finally to a desired goal or a special city. In other words, ask yourself what other stories you might have read that have a form something like this one. (If you want to think more about this before reading Revelation, turn to the end of the commentary for Chapter 22.)

(4) Think of a stage and all of its apparatus. Imagine John as the playwright. On stage is the drama of the historical events challenging the first-century church. Backstage is God, who knows the true meaning of those events and who wants the players on stage to understand them as well.

The stage setting, seen by the Christians, is the Greek

culture and the Roman government. Because of that, the players interpret the events as though they were all caused by and controlled by the Greeks and Romans.

John's book puts up new scenery. He decorates the stage with important symbols from the Old Testament, symbols that remind the players that God controls history. He puts up scenes of great natural devastation, far beyond what humans could do, to call attention to the God of the Creation. The real meaning of history, he wants them to see, comes not from Rome but from God.

As you read Revelation, remember that it was first read by people who saw only evidence of Roman power and success. They needed to see scenes that reminded them of God's essential role in history.

(5) Imagine yourself in a time of historical duress, in the presence of great temptation and evil. What assurances would you want? What signs would you look for? How would you console and encourage your fellow Christians or your children? Which images and stories from your religious tradition would you call on to remind them and yourself that history belongs to God and that it is important to keep the faith? In other words, imagine yourself in the position of John or his readers.

(6) Read the book through without worrying about the precise meaning of all of its signs and symbols. Keep track of its cumulative effect on yourself. Pay special attention to the effects of such passages as Revelation 21:3-4: *Behold, the dwelling of God is with men. He will dwell with them, and they shall be his people, and God himself shall be with them; he will wipe away every tear from their eyes, and death shall be no more, neither shall there be mourning nor crying nor pain any more, for the former things have passed away.*

(7) Read this book as though it were a series of stories. Don't try at first to force connections. Let the stories

stand on their own; think about them; see what connections emerge in your mind.

(8) Don't force premature conclusions about what the book means. Some think it is a detailed prediction of the course of human history. Others think it is a dramatic collection of stories and teachings meant to encourage Christians at all times to be faithful. Others think other things. Christians throughout history have produced a great variety of approaches to this book. So, don't feel rushed to come up with the definitive interpretation.

Revelation 1:1-8

Introduction to These Verses

A prologue is a brief introduction. In ancient drama, a small speech or event occurred on stage to alert the audience to the significance of the play they would soon see. John uses his prologue to set the stage for the letters, stories, and parables he plans to present.

In the prologue, John tells about the source of his message (an angel), the content and urgency of his message (*what must soon take place*), and the recipients of his message (the seven churches of Asia Minor).

Several words that are important to the Book of Revelation are mentioned for the first time in the prologue: *revelation, witness, angel, spirit,* the number *seven,* and the Greek words *alpha* and *omega.*

Those words will be explained as they appear in the verses of Revelation. It is well to be alerted now that John has several words that he uses frequently. Their meaning becomes clearer as they occur throughout the book.

The prologue has two parts:
 I. The Source of John's Message (1:1-3)
 II. Greetings to the Seven Churches (1:4-8)

The Source of John's Message (1:1-3)

Although the book is often referred to as the revelation of John, the first sentence puts it clearly: this is the revelation of Jesus Christ told to John by an angel. Further, the revelation of Jesus Christ is one that God gave to him. Christ revealed *what must soon take place.*

Now, through an angel, the message is given to John. The word *angel* means *messenger*, a divine messenger.

A revelation is the unveiling of a secret. In this case, God shows John the secret of what will happen in human history. Many in the early church believed that history would soon come to an end. That is, in part, the meaning of the "secret" revealed to John.

John calls himself a *witness to the word of God*. *Witness* may also be translated *martyr*, as it is later in the book when it refers to those who witnessed to Jesus and paid for it with suffering and, for some, death. A witness is one who has seen, or heard, the church's testimony about Jesus. It is also one who tells what has been seen. John is a witness in both of those senses.

John's letter brings blessings with it to all who read it and remain true to its message. Verse 3 is the first of seven blessings in the Book of Revelation. The others are in 14:13; 16:15; 19:9; 20:6; 22:7; 22:14.

The revelation (unveiling), therefore, is God's uncovering of what has been hidden. John receives it in order to tell the church. In it he passes on the secret about what is to happen soon.

John's reference to *he who reads aloud* tells us that he expected his words to be used in a worship or liturgical setting. Usually the books read in early Christian worship were from the Old Testament. Very likely, in the manner of the synagogue, a person was nominated to read either by the presbyters or the president. Very early, the reader became an official and a member of the clergy.

John also speaks of the *time being near*. In Greek there were two words for *time*. One referred to the normal passage of time—the daily, humdrum ticking away of the moments. The other referred to times that were fraught with significance. Here it is not just ordinary time, but the time for something to happen. It might be called "event time." John is not announcing that time routinely marches on; he announces a decisive moment.

Greetings to the Seven Churches (1:4-8)

There were more than seven churches in Asia Minor. The number seven had symbolic significance, meaning *all*, *complete*, or *perfect*. The seven churches were important in themselves, but they also stand for all of the church. What afflicted them afflicted the entire church. What was promised them was promised the entire church.

John does not identify himself further. He and his plight must have been known widely enough among the churches that they could recognize him by first name and by the kind of book he wrote. His interest in apocalyptic books would have placed him in the midst of Christians with similar interests. John gives this part of his book the form of a letter, a common form of religious and instructional writing.

John refers to God as *one who is and who was and who is to come*. Jewish Christians would recognize this immediately as a reference to Exodus 3:14, where God is revealed to Moses as *I AM WHO I AM*, or *I WILL BE WHAT I WILL BE*. The God who will be coming soon is the same God who has been creator of the Jewish nation and of the church.

The promise of grace and peace is more than a passing comment or a casual greeting. Under the influence of Paul, the early church would understand *grace* to mean the favor of God, now given especially through Jesus Christ. *Peace* is the harmony that Christ restored between God and people. The phrase *Grace to you and peace* occurs in nine of Paul's letters. It may have become a brief, common expression of the profoundest hopes of the early believers.

The *seven spirits* again emphasizes the symbolic meaning of the number seven. They may mean the full or complete Spirit of God.

Verses 5 and 6 summarize a great deal of New Testament belief. Christ freed believers by his death and made them a kingdom of priests. That overturns Greek and Roman ideas about kingdoms based on power and wealth. The kingdom of God is made up of those who are priests of God to each other. It is therefore justice and service that define the true meaning of the word *kingdom*.

The message to the churches is from God, the Spirit, and Jesus Christ. The reference to Jesus as *first-born of the dead* and *ruler of the kings on earth* mattered greatly to those who saw their friends die, and themselves faced death at the hands of those earthly rulers who seemed to be the kings of the earth. God's kingship is now hidden to the world, but revealed to the faithful.

God's kingship reaches beyond national boundaries; it has global significance. It will be revealed to all, to the detriment of those who harmed God, either directly or by harming God's people.

The small word *amen* in verse 7 has a very large meaning for John. He uses it at the close of prayers (7:12), for accepting as one's own what another has said (5:14), and as a name for Christ (3:14). It means *it is so*. In regard to Christ, then, it means that he is the one who guarantees that what he says is so.

Alpha and *Omega* are the first and last letters of the Greek alphabet, the language in which John wrote. Like the Hebrew *aleph* and *tau* and the English *a* to *z*, it means the beginning and the end or the first and the last. The beginning and the end, and all that lies in between, belong to God. The saying especially emphasizes that history has an end, in both senses of that word. It has a goal toward which it drives. And it has a conclusion—it will not last forever.

In these verses, John's sharp sense of the closeness of the end, of the inevitability of judgment, and of the universality of God, provide the theme for the entire book. The remaining chapters spell out, through sermons and parables, what it means.

§ § § § § § §

The Message of Revelation 1:1-8

Revelation means to remove the veil, to make visible something that has been hidden. Christ, although hidden from the nations (even though it is through their own blindness that they cannot see him), has been revealed to John. John is to be a prophet and witness, to tell what he has seen. His message is to be read aloud in the seven churches of Asia Minor. The number seven is a symbol for completeness or totality. The letters, therefore, are to be read to all of the churches. What does the prologue affirm?

§ That God has been revealed through prophets and angels;

§ That God has continued to be known through Christ, who gave John the message of Revelation;

§ That Christ is the ruler over all the earth;

§ That God is eternal (the alpha and omega);

§ That we are a kingdom and all priests of God.

§ § § § § § §

Revelation 1:9-20

Introduction to These Verses

In this part, John tells what happened to him as he received the first vision recorded in his book. He also demonstrates his familiarity with important Jewish symbols—something that would give his work authority with the early Christians, many of whom were converted Jews. It would have meant a good deal to all Christians, however, because the Old Testament was the only Bible of the early church. But most of all, he shows how those traditional symbols could be turned to the service of the Christian church.

John speaks in this part of receiving his message while he was *in this Spirit on the Lord's day*. We do not know precisely what kind of an experience that was or how much of his message came to him at that time. In Revelation, he intermingles reports of visions with interpretations and with warnings to his readers to pay attention.

Reports of spellbinding experiences are not rare in the Bible. Nor are books or actions based on visions.

Here is an outline of Revelation 1:9-20.
  I. The Call and the Command (1:9-11)
 II. The One *Like a Son of Man* (1:12-16)
III. An Order and an Explanation (1:17-20)

The Call and the Command (1:9-11)

Verse 9 contains three key terms: *tribulation, kingdom,* and *patient endurance.* Those who waited for God's kingdom and were loyal to it could not give their loyalty to kingdoms of this earth. Rome, however, under the rule of Domitian, aggressively sought not only the loyalty but the worship of Roman subjects. Christians could not comply. Hence, tribulation.

Tribulation comes from the earlier word *tribulum*, which is a wooden platform laced with studs made of sharp nails and cleats. Grain was poured upon it and beaten. The word not only makes vivid the individual suffering that some Christians endured. It also presents a harsh image of the historical period. This was a time of threshing and of separating the wheat from the chaff.

Tribulation created the need for patient endurance. The word *patience* relates to the word *passion*, as in our Lord's passion; it means to suffer, to have bad things done to you, not simply have them happen to you.

To endure means to remain firm, and comes from an earlier word meaning *hard*. Christians must remain firm in the fury of tribulation.

The message of Revelation contained in these words, then, is: "The present age has inflicted pain and death on us and will continue to do so. Don't give in; accept the pain and remain firmly loyal to God's kingdom."

John had undergone what the others had, and paid for it with his exile to Patmos. Preaching had gotten him into trouble.

John speaks about the island of Patmos in the past tense. He is therefore writing from memory, some time after the events he records in his book. Patmos is one of the Sporades Islands off the coast of the southwest tip of Asia Minor. It is a barren and rocky island ten miles in length and five miles wide. It was one of many that Rome used as penal colonies. Records show that Domitian, the emperor during the time of John's imprisonment, banished several persons to the islands.

Islands like Patmos imprisoned two kinds of offenders, and had two kinds of punishment. However, there were some things in common for all. First, the punishment was regarded as banishment, which meant that, for most persons, it was life-long. (John, however, writes, as we have noticed, in the past tense, indicating that he was among the fortunate few to leave the island.) Second, the punishment included a total loss of one's civil rights and the loss of nearly all of one's property.

That is where the similarities ended. Some exiles were allowed to move freely throughout the island, to earn small amounts of money, and to conduct their lives without undergoing physical punishment or cruelty. The empire tended to treat prisoners from families of wealth and high standing with that kind of tolerance.

Less fortunate exiles experienced quite a different fate. For them, Rome reserved many of the physical nightmares we have seen visualized in films: hard labor, chains, ragged and insufficient clothing, meager food, scourging, and exhaustion. No money was earned, and accommodations were, at the most, small spaces on the dirt floors of dark prisons.

John may well have been one of those less fortunate exiles. He calls himself one who shares the *tribulation* and the *patient endurance*. His exile took place during the time of Domitian, when the penalty for being a Christian could be death. Christians were punished by fire, crucifixion, or being used in the bloody spectacles at festivals and games. Tradition has it that both Paul and Peter died at the hands of the government.

On the Lord's day (either Saturday or Sunday), John was *in the Spirit*. John shows by that statement that he is in the line of prophets reaching back through the major prophets of the Jewish Scriptures. They too testified that God had spoken to them through deep and absorbing religious experiences.

Many think that the *Lord's day* mentioned by John must be Sunday. In Asia Minor there was a tradition in the early church for referring to Sunday as the Lord's day. It fit with the inherited pattern of Jewish practice of the time to have a special day for worship and study each week. The Jewish day, however, began with sundown on Friday and concluded at sundown Saturday. Christians moved to the first day of the week because it commemorated the day of Jesus' resurrection.

It was not in the Jewish tradition, though, to call their special day the Lord's day. That custom may have arisen to counteract a Roman practice. From before the Christian era, Asia Minor and Egypt both called the first day of the month "Emperor's Day," asserting the Emperor's dominance over land and people. Christians, who believed heartily in God's ownership of land, people, and time, claimed not the first of the month, but the first of every week as the Lord's day.

Some scholars believe that the choice of the phrase *Lord's day* for the first of the week became very popular among apocalyptic groups. They were the ones who accented most strongly the difference between the powers of this age and the power of God. Each service of worship on the Lord's day brought them reassurance that, ultimately, the world belonged to God, not to the emperor.

The Judaism John knew was the form practiced in Palestine during and after Jesus' life. The early Christian church grew out of, and transformed, that tradition. But it kept Judaism's lively sense of the Spirit. The Spirit grants the gift of prophecy. It is also what God gives the righteous to help them endure and keep their moral resolve. Further, in the last days, the Jews believed, the messiah would have the Spirit to bolster and renew the faithful.

John reports hearing a loud voice, telling him to write a letter to the seven churches in Asia Minor. Probably these seven were selected because they represented most of the possible problems facing the young church at the time. People in John's day would recognize the special meaning of the number seven, indicating "all" or "completeness."

The voice commands John to write what he sees and to send it in a letter to the churches. In Rome and in the early church a letter had great stature. Teaching, advice, philosophy, and directions might all find their place in a letter, as they did in the letters of the apostle Paul. John's letters, then, fit into an already established tradition, and would have commanded a hearing in the churches.

The seven churches of Asia Minor were seven postal districts, and were also tribunal cities (cities in which laws were administered and trials were held). Each sat strategically on a great circular route which connected them with each other and served as a major artery for commerce.

The One *Like a Son of Man* (1:12-16)

John's readers would have recognized this description immediately. The seven gold lampstands (from Zechariah 4:1-10) would have reminded them of the menorah, the seven-branched candlestick that stood in the Temple to symbolize the unity of God. (The menorah could also symbolize the seven days of Creation.)

One *like a son of man* would have stirred strong recollections of the writings of the prophet Daniel (Daniel 7:9-14 and 10:16). Many Christians took Daniel's description of the Son of man as a forecast of Jesus. Jesus had used that phrase often, although not always clearly pointing it at himself. But he did use the phrase as both Daniel and John did, referring to one who would come at the end of time, one who would usher in the day of justice.

The description of the voice echoes words from the Jewish tradition, especially Ezekiel 1:24 and 43:2. To those who were in the know, John's images signified that Christ was the source of the messages in the letters, just as the presence of lights and ornaments signify to us not simply a pine tree, but a Christmas tree.

John's description of the one *like a son of man* shows his

skill in bringing together ideas and images from his own library of resources. The garment he wears (verse 13) is that of a high priest. The golden belt was worn by royalty. He has many things in common with the angel seen by Daniel: the golden belt, flaming eyes, legs and feet shining like bronze. The flaming eyes symbolize great and penetrating knowledge.

The importance of the reference to bronze can be seen if one contrasts it with the image Daniel describes in Daniel 2:33. There Daniel describes to the king a vision of an image of silver and bronze, but with feet of clay. The image stands for the king and kingdom of Babylon. In Daniel's vision, the image is destroyed; its feet of clay crumble. John sees one whose feet are like burnished bronze (verse 15).

The description of the *one like a son of man* draws together elements from the entire creation. From the earth come snow and fire; from human beings come the head and eyes; from the realm of inanimate materials come water and bronze; from the heavens come the stars and the sun. In John's religious tradition, each of these had been transformed into a religious symbol. It is the symbolic meaning, not the literal description, that he is drawing from his library to help him describe the meaning of his own vision. Within the fellowship of those to whom John wrote, those symbols would have confirmed that the old beliefs are fulfilled in Jesus.

The *two-edged sword* was a traditional symbol of justice which, when it is true, cuts evenly from either side. The one like a Son of man brings, not arbitrary judgments, but justice. John will soon explain about the seven stars.

An Order and an Explanation (1:17-20)

Visions of God are overwhelming. Daniel fell in a faint, Jeremiah and Ezekiel both fell to the ground and worshiped, and Isaiah feared for his life. John falls at the foot of the vision as though he were dead.

The *one like a son of man* touches John and assures him that he is the risen Lord, using words that echo 1:8—he is the first and the last (the alpha and omega), but also the one who died and is now alive. The keys to heaven and Hell rest in the hands of the risen Christ. Near the end of his revelation, John will see the doors to death and Hell closed and sealed, finally and forever, under the authority of the Risen Lord. The notion of *keys* appears elsewhere in the New Testament, always with the idea of the power and authority to execute judgment and justice.

John is ordered to write. In order to place the letters to the churches in their proper perspective, he explains his vision. The one like a Son of man stands in the midst of seven lampstands, seven stars nested in his hand, and the two-edged sword issuing from his mouth. This is a highly symbolic vision. The lampstands are the seven churches (seven means the entire church) and the seven stars are the angels of those churches.

The word *angel* means *one who is sent* or *messenger*. But here the meaning is greater. As John demonstrates throughout the entire book, the connections between heaven and earth are quite close. Many things spread in their existence through both places, like a house on the boundary between two states. The churches on earth have their angels and live on the boundary that crosses from Asia Minor over into the very hand of God.

But why should letters, many of which are critical, be sent to a church that resides already partly in God's hand? As John shows later in the book, both heaven and earth required redemption. He will speak later about strife between the powers of good and evil in heaven itself. And, when God brings the present age to its close, John envisions both a new earth and a new heaven (21:1).

John has no doubt he is writing to the seven churches about the need to endure in the midst of strife that is not only earthly, but cosmic in extent.

34   REVELATION

John uses the word *mystery* in verse 20. Mystery, in the New Testament, is not a "who-done-it." It means something that humans could not know or learn by themselves. Here Christ makes known the meanings of symbols that the Christians could not understand on their own.

Mystery comes from the Greek word meaning *to keep silent*. It seldom has to do with strange or eerie events. God's mystery is God's secret. But even after a revelation the secret is not entirely known; God's revelation provides information and guidance, but also the promise that more will come clear in the future.

§ § § § § § §

The Message of Revelation 1:9-20

John tells about his imprisonment on the island of Patmos. There, on the Lord's Day, he is told to write a message to the seven churches. The message he writes comes from *one like a son of man* (a traditional figure in Old Testament writings, but one whom Christians took to refer to the crucified and risen Christ). What is the meaning of John's vision of *one like a son of man*?

§ Christ is in the midst of the church.
§ Christ is pure and powerful, and will bring justice.
§ Death and Hell will not have the final word in the lives of believers. Christ holds the key to them both.
§ Prophecy concerns both what is and what is to come.
§ The church of Christ extends from earth into heaven.

§ § § § § § §

PART THREE Revelation 2:1-17

Introduction to These Verses

The letter was an important form of communication in the ancient world. Archaeologists have found evidences of many different kinds of letters. One kind most frequently found is the instructional letter: one that gives advice, teaches, or offers information on important topics.

One reason for the popularity of letters is that, during the first century A.D., the ancient world achieved a very high level of literacy. A much greater percentage of the population could read than was able to during the Middle Ages. Some scholars say there were more readers in first-century Rome than at any time until the modern age.

Christian literature features many letters. Paul's New Testament writings are all letters. But other Christians wrote them as well. We have many examples from bishops and church leaders from throughout the early centuries. When John chose to put part of his book in the form of letters, he knew he had selected a literary form that his readers knew and would take seriously.

John's letters may have been written independently of one another and have been sent to the churches. It is clear that John knew the circumstances of each of the congregations to which he wrote. If he did write each letter separately (perhaps while a prisoner), he later collected them for his book. The Book of Revelation, as John indicated in 1:9-10, was written after his time in Patmos. The letters were written under the inspiration of a mighty vision. When John wrote about his vision in its entirety, the letters may have then been restored and put in their place among the visions and inspirations from Patmos.

The order of the letters to the seven churches is no accident. Ephesus, the first mentioned, lies closest to the island of Patmos. Smyrna, the next, rests to the north. From there on, the route connecting these large cities of Asia Minor forms a loop—roughly, the very path one would take traveling on foot to deliver mail. Clearly, John knew the main travel arteries of the area.

He knew the cities and their churches, as well. Each letter he writes speaks directly to the condition of the church and to the mischief caused by its environment.

The letters all tend to have the same pattern:

(1) A statement from the Lord which includes some part of the vision from 1:12-16;

(2) Praise for what is good and criticism for what is wrong with each congregation (although Sardis and Laodicea receive no praise and Smyrna and Philadelphia receive no criticism);

(3) A promise made to those who endure;

(4) A plea to listen to the Spirit's message.

John refers often to those who endure tribulation as *conquerors* and speaks frequently of their crowns. There were two words for crown. One, similar to our word *diadem*, referred to the royal crown and was a symbol of power. The other, the one promised the conquerors, is a wreath of the sort awarded to the victor at games (those who endured to the end).

The coastal churches had the advantage of receiving commercial goods from land and sea. They also caught all of the lastest gossip, fads, and fancies from everywhere. Each was a cosmopolitan center, welcoming people from every city and shore and used to entertaining ideas from everywhere in the ancient world. All of them housed important temples, and each surrounded Christians with the temptation to average out religious faiths rather than remain committed to one. John, in his letters, addresses those temptations head on.

Here is an outline of Revelation 2.

I. The Letter to Ephesus (2:1-7)
II. The Letter to Smyrna (2:8-11)
III. The Letter to Pergamum (2:12-17)

The Letter to Ephesus (2:1-7)

Ephesus was a seaport and one of the great cities of the ancient world. It was rich and politically very important, housing as it did the Roman proconsul for Asia Minor. More important, from John's point of view, it also housed the temple of the goddess Artemis (her temple was one of the seven wonders of the ancient world), the energetic worship of the Roman emperor and empire, and a lively belief in magic among the citizens.

Merge wealth, power, magic, and competing religions, and they create an environment that taxes the faith and obedience of Christians. Add to that several flare-ups, popular and military, against Jews and Jewish Christians, and the temptations increase. Surrounded by symbols of how agreeable and endlessly interesting the secular world can be, yet forced to keep their distance from it, Christians become grudging and cool. Resentment dissolves love.

The message to Ephesus comes from him who stands in the midst of John's vision. It praises the church's endurance, its ability to identify and weed out false apostles, and its patience. The church's love, however, has dwindled—the essential ingredient of the Christian life (1 Corinthians 13). The Ephesians are reminded that, if they lack love, they gain nothing.

The threat John makes to the Ephesians is severe. He says, in verse 5, that they must repent of their lovelessness or be removed. To a congregation that had known Paul and now sensed itself as the leading church among the Christians, the threat would have been shocking. Evidently the Ephesians heeded John's warning, for the church remained for some time the leader in Asian Christianity. Some years later, the bishop of Ephesus was acknowledged to be the head of the Asian church.

Verse 7 records a promise to the conquerors. It is a word John uses often. The notion that the Christian life is a form of warfare occurs elsewhere in the Bible. For John, the combat between God and evil was relentless. The military image of conquering and of warfare would be all too familiar to a people who lived under military domination and had seen their homeland destroyed. John holds out the promise that even the least of them can endure and be a conqueror.

John speaks of the *toil* of the Ephesians. Toil comes from a Greek word meaning "to labor to the point of weariness or exhaustion." It derives its meaning from the word for *beating* or the physical tiredness that comes from the repeated impact of manual labor. Literally, then, when John speaks of the toil of the Christians, he gives us a clue to the extreme demands placed on them. To be faithful exacts great stress; Christians working for the church work to the point of exhaustion.

To their credit, the Ephesians recognize and spurn the Nicolaitans. Who the Nicolaitans were—other than followers of Nicholas, as their name implies—is not known. They may have been one of the many groups that taught permissive Christianity; especially those that taught that, if one truly believed in Christ, one could indulge in promiscuous sex or pagan religion without sin.

Those who promise to endure through the good times as well as the bad will eat from the tree of life. The tree of life is an important symbol from the Old Testament story of the garden of Eden. The tree and other items from that story appear again in the final chapter of Revelation.

The tree of life symbolizes immortality. Only those who have conquered may eat of it. John knows that, for some, the struggle to endure may become a life or death issue. He therefore lifts their sights beyond the immediate to the eternal promise. He does here, as he often does, change the scenery in which people act out their lives, replacing the seen with the unseen, the visible threats with the invisible truths.

John's use of the tree also shows how he was able to transform the symbols of other religions, and to convert them to a Christian use. Trees had been worshiped as the homes of divine beings or as places where the divine being might be made apparent. Families had sacred trees, which they thought were closely linked with family prosperity. The Greeks had kept certain groves of trees as sacred places. When the Acropolis of Athens had been burned and the people feared for their future, the sacred olive tree put forth a new shoot. The people had taken that as a sign that the future would go well for them. Trees growing over the graves of the dead were thought to carry the life and spirit of the departed one. There is even evidence of an old Athenian law that prescribed punishment for those who cut certain kinds of trees down from cemeteries.

John was writing to Christians who had been born and raised in the midst of the Greek and Roman culture. The mysteries of nature, the kinship of trees to gods and goddesses and families, the tranquility and worship inspired by the sacred groves—all were familiar features of their environment. John knows that. He uses it now for a wider meaning, changing the scenery, as we have noted, to place the tree now in the Garden of Eden, and its meaning in the hope held for the faithful.

The Letter to Smyrna (2:8-11)

Smyrna was also a seaport and therefore a rich and powerful city. John contrasts the city to Christ and Christians.

Smyrna, in 195 B.C., had dedicated a temple to the

goddess of Rome. In A.D. 26 it erected a temple to the emperor Tiberius and to the Roman senate. Smyrna competed with Ephesus to be known as the first among the cities of Asia. John, by contrast, wrote for a Christ who was not only first, but last as well. Smyrna was a rich city, but the true riches, according to John, belong to Christians. The city of Smyrna was bedecked with large buildings and temples, referred to as the crown of Smyrna, but John's Christ promises Christians the crown of life.

John speaks of knowing the poverty of the church at Smyrna. He uses the strong form of the Greek word for poverty. It is not that the Christians at Smyrna had nothing extra; they had almost nothing at all.

The letter warns of a time of suffering and of an imprisonment lasting *ten days*. Some of the suffering was caused by Jewish settlers and citizens whose hostility to the Christians continued throughout the century. Imprisonment, however, was a governmental act. One stayed in prison while awaiting trial. For many Christians, the outcome of such trials led directly to death and, promises John, the *crown of life*.

John's reference to the *synagogue of Satan* shows that the Christians at Smyrna felt themselves to be fighting for survival on two fronts. There was a large Jewish settlement there, and the hostility between Jews and Christians continued throughout the first century. The situation was worsened by the fact that many of the Christians were converted Jews, some former members of the local synagogues.

John charges the Jews with slandering the Christians. It is true that Jews did take part in some of the persecutions. John's defense is twofold. He claims that Christians are the true Jews—it is they who will receive the crown of life. And he claims that the Jewish synagogue is an expression of evil, not of God.

Part of John's anger at the Jews may arise from the fact

that he himself is a Jewish Christian and has weaned himself from the life of the synagogue. Conversion to Christianity also meant being rejected by the Jewish community.

When John uses the phrase *crown of life*, he again illustrates how familiar parts of the local environment can be called into the service of his message. The phrase *crown of Smyrna* was common to his readers. The city's buildings, as mentioned above, were considered its crown, its diadem. But crowns were also familiar features of social and religious life. Worshipers of the pagan gods wore crowns of garlands or circlets of flowers. Laurel wreaths were given to the winners of athletic events.

The city of Smyrna had also been compared to the crown of Ariadne. That association would be more important and more compelling for John. In Greek myth, Ariadne had been romanced and then abandoned by Theseus. As Ariadne wept, Venus (the diety of love) came to console Ariadne. Venus also promised her that she would be the bride of Bacchus. She was given a golden crown, placed among the stars, and bore Bacchus a son.

That story was closely associated with religious beliefs that permitted promiscuity. The crown, then, spoke volumes about things that John knew threatened Christian belief—worldly power, pagan religion, and promiscuity. Those may have seemed to some to offer life. He knew the true *crown of life* came from elsewhere and was offered by someone else.

The crown of life also has a relationship to the crowns of light (also called *nimbuses*) that appear in the works of art depicting Greek dieties. Those crowns, which we now call *halos*, very soon showed up in Christian art as well. Those crowns were quickly associated with the blessed. This is, possibly, a testimony to the ability of John and others to transform their environment into eloquent symbols of the faith.

The *one who died and came to life* promises Christians who conquer all temptations and who face death that the second death, presumably the one following resurrection and judgment, will not hurt them. John uses the phrase *second death* four times. It does not appear elsewhere in the New Testament. It appears again in Revelation 20:6 where John says that those who reign with Christ during the Millennium will not experience the second death. It is referred to also in Chapters 20 and 21 when the enemies of God are cast into the lake of fire.

The idea of a second death was familiar to the Jews, and probably to John's readers. It helps to distinguish between a death that all must suffer and one that must be suffered only by those who do not receive the benefits of the resurrection.

The *crown of life* is what makes the difference between the two. Those who endure the first death in faith achieve a crown more glorious than the one that bedecks Smyrna, one that will not tarnish. It is more glorious than the crown of Ariadne, for she only dwells among the stars. The crown of life is given by him who holds the stars in his hands.

The Letter to Pergamum (2:12-17)

Pergamum was the capital of the Roman province of Asia. It was built upon a thousand-foot hill, on which were both temples and the acropolis—a fortress protecting the city. It housed many religious movements alongside its temple dedicated to Caesar Augustus and Rome. Many coins of the era carried pictures of the temple. The imperial cult (the official religion) had its Asian center in Pergamum.

When John refers to Christ as the one with the *two-edged sword*, he is contrasting the power of God's truth to the power of Roman military might. The hill on which the acropolis sat, with its solid and nearly invincible setting and its decorative assortment of temples, John calls *Satan's throne*. Those who remained faithful to Christ in the midst of all of these symbols of power often paid with their lives as Antipas had. Rome's power took its toll on Christians.

The faithful were called *witnesses*, for which another term is *martyrs*. *Martyr* soon came to stand for those in the early church who told what they had seen and believed about Christ, and who paid the ultimate price: death.

Some Christians at Pergamum had fallen, not to death, but to the practices of other religions. John refers to the *teaching of Balaam* (see Numbers 31:8), an enemy of Israel who believed that the Israelites would lose God's protection if they could be persuaded to worship idols.

A *stumbling block* is the stick that holds the bait in a bird trap. Once a bird perches on the stick, the trap springs. What were the Christian's stumbling blocks? Eating food sacrificed to idols (which led other, weaker persons to think Christians could also worship idols), immorality, and following the teachings of the Nicolaitans.

Those who remain faithful will receive three rewards: (1) *hidden manna*, from the mysterious food by which God fed the Israelites in the desert following their escape from Egypt and the Pharaoh. Now the new Moses, Christ, will provide even more. (2) A *white stone*. After a jury trial in Roman courts, the defendant would receive either a white stone (innocent) or a black one (guilty). In some cases, the stone meant literally life or death. Believers will gain life. (3) A *new name*. Names, in the ancient world, not only referred to a person, they described character. A new name meant a new character, the new person Christ would make out of those who remained faithful.

Names appeared on white stones for another reason in the ancient world. There was a popular superstition that certain mysterious names carried special powers. Followers of some religions carried white stones (called amulets) engraved either with religious names or magical formulas. If the name on the amulet were new, and known only to the holder, the value of it increased enormously. If others learned the name or formula, they could also share in its powers.

John may have used that superstition as an analogy of what God does for the Christian. That is, the new name given believers will not be understood by the world, but it will be a symbol of the power of God to see that person through tribulation and into God's kingdom.

The word *new* is very important in Revelation. The book contains references to a new name, a new Jerusalem, and a new heaven and earth. The word has a special sense. It refers not only to something that is recent, that is new by virtue of its only having recently arrived. In that sense, the new, when it arrives, may be not much different from the old. The word John uses means *fresh*—a matter of a change in quality. It usually implies *better*.

§ § § § § § §

The Message of Revelation 2:1-17

In this part, John addresses the churches in the cities
on the western coast of Asia Minor. Some of the
Christians there have faced pain and imprisonment; all
have had to deal with temptations. Some temptations
have arisen because the world had filled those cities with
enticing novelty. Other temptations arose because of
doctrines distorted by members of the church. In the
wake of those pressures within and without, John sends
the following messages:

§ God knows the circumstances faced by every church
and every Christian.

§ In spite of all trials and temptations, Christians must
remain loving and faithful.

§ The Christian life is like an endurance race; one must
prepare for the long haul.

§ Some temptations appear new, but they have been
around a long time in one form or another; most of them
are forms of a single temptation: to accommodate to the
surrounding culture.

§ God's promises are longstanding, too; and God will
be true to those promises and to all who remain faithful.

§ God will strengthen Christians in their times of need
and trial.

§ § § § § § §

PART FOUR Revelation 2:18–3:22

Introduction to These Chapters

The inland churches were not spared either strife or temptation. Three of the four had yielded. One, Thyatira, while generally faithful, had begun a kind of loose-minded tolerance. Its acceptance of a woman named Jezebel signaled not so much a love-inspired openness as an unexamined doctrinal error. Jezebel taught falsely. The idolatry of behavior she inspired led from the way she twisted basic beliefs. Thyatira needed sounder teaching.

Sardis, too, erred because it forgot what it had been taught. Its beliefs forgotten, its works wandered down dangerous pathways. In truth, this hyperactive church spun its wheels in unproductive activity.

Laodicea had wandered farthest. It had turned the faith completely upside down, taking on worldly values, baptizing them, and pretending that that made them Christian. Again, a failing in behavior stemmed from a breakdown of careful thought.

Only Philadelphia, whose name means *city of love*, received John's praise. Even there, doctrinal issues are at hand, but so far Philadelphia has kept both its heart and its head pure.

The inland churches did not face the welter of novelty that nearly engulfed the coastal churches. But they did not escape problems. For the most part, those problems arose from the entrenched societies of their cities: craft guilds, popular temples, families of great prestige and influence who set the social standards and had done so

48   REVELATION for generations. Old wealth and power, in spite of the new Roman control, still set much of the stage on which the early church played its first roles in history. And the church had trouble with them as much as it did with new wealth and power. It is difficult to feel secure with a new faith when one is surrounded with contrary institutions that seem to have stood the test of time.

Here is an outline of Revelation 2:18–3:22.

I. The Letter to Thyatira (2:18-29)
II. The Letter to Sardis (3:1-6)
III. The Letter to Philadelphia (3:7-13)
IV. The Letter to Laodicea (3:14-22)

The Letter to Thyatira (2:18-29)

Though it was not the key city in Asia, Thyatira had a thriving business in crafts and trades. As a result, it had numerous trade guilds, among them wool-workers, garment-makers, dyers, leather-workers, tanners, potters, bakers, slave-dealers, and bronze-smiths. Luke, in Acts, names a Lydia who came from Thyatira and was a seller of purple.

Guilds each related to their own gods as well as to the official religion of Rome. Guild meetings could end in worship, drunkenness, sexual license, or all three. For Christians, earning a living through membership in a guild became a crisis of conscience.

Experience with those trades allowed John to forge some very appropriate symbols in his letter to the church at Thyatira. Those close to the metal workers, for example, would know the importance of burnished brass to warfare, where its highly reflective surface was used to deflect the sun's light and blind the enemy. Here, in a city that prided itself on blinding its enemies, John describes a *Son of God* who, never blinded, sees through one's heart like a fire burning, whose gaze cuts into places others cannot see at all.

The church in Thyatira has been faithful in love and

service, and has even improved. But in its midst is a Jezebel. The original Jezebel was the wife of Ahab; her name became proverbial among the Jews for wickedness, much as Hitler's name has become for our age. The woman in Thyatira has great power and is thought by some in that church to be a prophet, like John. But, in fact, she lures Christians into eating meats given to idols—possibly at guild banquets—and into submitting bit by bit to the practices of pagan cults.

The problem of eating food sacrificed to idols (verse 20) was complicated. The early church had honest differences about it. To those who knew God as revealed in Jesus Christ, it was clear that idols were nothing. Consequently, food sacrificed to idols was simply food, nothing more. Most of the guilds had their gods, and when a common meal of guild members was held, food was sacrificed, then eaten. Add to that the dilemma of the Christian who needed guild membership in order to practice a trade, and the eating of such food must have seemed both harmless (to the true Christian) and necessary (to be sociable within the guild). Paul had held that eating such food was, in principle, all right. However, if it led the weaker members of the church to misunderstand and then to believe that worship of idols was allowed, it must be avoided. John does not allow such latitude. It is possible that he disallowed it because it was being supported by Jezebel, whose total doctrine was dangerous. Thus, to give in on one point meant to give the impression that she might be right on others.

The judgment announced by John is wrenching. The reclining bed used for festive dinners with others (guild meals, perhaps) becomes a sickbed for them all. The Christians who follow her must repent or else face the dire fate she faces. What Jezebel announces as the deep things of God, John reveals to be, in truth, the deep things of Satan.

In verses 22-23, John distinguishes between two kinds

of followers of Jezebel. Some have been lured by her gradually into wider participation in the pagan cults associated with their guilds. For them, John holds out the hope of repentance. Others, her *children*, have fully adopted Jezebel's teachings. For them John pronounces the severest judgment.

To the rest of the Christians at Thyatira, the Son of man promises no more burdens. Their circumstances will be reversed. They, the weak, will have power over the nations. They will be able to shatter resistance to the work of the Son of man. God promises them the morning star, Venus—in ancient times a symbol of sovereignty.

The word translated *rule* literally means *to shepherd*. This is not an image of meekness. Shepherds ruled their flocks with strength and absolute control, breaking away threats, although for the ultimate welfare of the flock.

The Letter to Sardis (3:1-6)

Sardis was an ancient city that had risen in splendor in 560 B.C. and had been in gradual decline ever since. It had great wealth, and its wealth made it irresponsible. Sardis had military might, and that might made it overconfident. Twice, despite its magnificent strategic position, enemies had scaled its walls at night and conquered the city. The guards, foolishly incautious, had left their posts.

John knows that history. He reminds the Christians at Sardis that his message comes from the one who holds seven spirits in his hand. In the early church, as in Judaism, the spirits are viewed as the sources by which God gives life and enlivens the living. The reference to the spirits contrasts with the city of Sardis and its church, who *have the name of being alive* but are dead.

Christians living in a city that had been twice captured by enemies in the dark of night would surely understand allusions to God's coming *like a thief in the night*. They must remain alert and watchful. Part of watchfulness is remembering. The Greek word for *remembering* means more than to entertain a past event in one's mind. It means to let that remembrance bear on one's behavior.

Robes of white symbolize holiness. They will be worn by those whose names remain in the book of life. Ancient cities used registration books to certify those who had the rights of citizenship. In this case, John reminds those who remain faithful that their names fill, not an earthly register, but God's book of life. In the soft and spoiled city of Sardis, the eventual and true victors are those who awaken, remember, and remain watchful.

John's reference to the *book of life* would have kindled recollections of different sorts among the Jewish and Greek Christians. Jewish religion used the notion of official lists in several ways. As early as Exodus there are records of official lists and of registrars to make them. Those lists determined who could share in the community's goods. One punishment greatly feared would be to have one's name removed from the list. It meant no more access to food and supplies—almost certainly death.

The *book of life* gradually came to mean, not the list of citizens of the nation, but of those who were citizens in God's kingdom. Several Jewish and New Testament writings speak of the opening of such books. And, again, to have one's name removed from the book is a grim sentence. But the more positive message is the one conveyed here: Those whose religion deprives them of the rights of earthly citizenship have their names inscribed elsewhere. They are not forgotten.

Greek and Roman cities of John's time also kept lists. Citizens' names were kept according to their class and family. The practice of keeping track of citizens can be seen in the story of Jesus' birth—Mary and Joseph being sent to the city of Bethlehem *because he was of the house . . . of David* (Luke 2:4). It was the Roman emperor Caesar Augustus who ordered that enrollment of all the people.

In Greek and Roman cities, all new citizens were entered into the records. And, when citizens violated the laws sufficiently, their names were erased. That erasure may have been the fate of those exiled to Patmos with John. In this case, a name on the book gave one the rights of citizenship and the protection of the community. Loss of those rights cost one, if not his life, very likely his livelihood.

Christians of either Greek or Jewish background, then, would know the deprivation of losing their place in the book. Those in Sardis needed especially to think of that. They had, in effect, traded one book for the other. Inscribing their names so willingly on the registry of secular ways had erased them from the book of life.

The white garments promised those who endure draw attention also to two different notions. Among the Romans, the typical holiday robe was white. On a day celebrating a military triumph, white was the universal color. Dark-colored robes were worn as signs of sorrow and mourning.

If white celebrates the Roman military conqueror, John can make it celebrate the Christian conqueror—the one who overcomes temptation. For him, white stands for purity, not worldly power. He will, later in the book, again depict the martyrs and the other faithful, dressed in white.

Once more, John shows how to take the familiar events about him and rescript them to speak in a new voice, with a new meaning. The military parade transforms into a pageant in heaven. The book of registry becomes a book of life. The conqueror becomes, not the one who overwhelms others, but one who overcomes temptation.

The Letter to Philadelphia (3:7-13)

Its founders expected to use Philadelphia as the gateway to spread the Greek language and culture throughout Asia. It housed many temples, including one to the god Dionysus. Jews had also settled there, and apparently the early church often found itself in conflict with them. John speaks of the Jewish community as Satan's synagogue, testifying to the degree of hostility between Jews and Christians in Philadelphia. Clearly, it was a city of ambition, tradition, religion, and ferment.

Verse 9 appears to promise the conversion of the Jews. John, as a Jewish Christian, believes not that Christianity is a new religion, but that it is the true religion of Abraham and Moses. It had wandered from its true origin. Now Christians represent the recovery of the true tradition. Anchoring that claim is John's deeper belief that it is not nationality but faith in Christ that makes one a true Jew. The irony here comes from John's knowledge of the Old Testament writings, especially the prophets, which promised that Israel would be a light to the nations and that kings would come to her to see the brightness of her rising. John says instead that Israel will come to the feet of the church to see the fullness of God's love. It is obvious from this and other passages of Revelation that the tensions between Christians and Jews were never far from the surface.

In a city with a proud tradition, John writes to remind the Christians that they too have a proud tradition. He connects them with David, anchoring the Christians' claim to be the true children of David and therefore the true Israel. In a city once conceived to be the gateway for spreading Greek culture, the small body of Christians know that, to whatever future really matters, it is Christ who holds the key. And Christ's key opens the door, not only to those now in God's kingdom, but to others, even enemies, who will enter into true worship.

In verse 12 John records a promise to the conquerors: They will be *pillars* in the temple of God. Those who still remembered the Temple in Jerusalem would find that a powerful promise, for that Temple had been the place of pilgrimages for centuries, until its destruction. It would also speak to those who had lived their lives in Rome or its provinces. The priest of the Roman imperial cult each year would erect his own statue in the temple devoted to worshiping the emperor. His name, place of birth, and year of office were recorded. Thus he obtained an enduring place in his temple. The Christians would be not statues, but pillars in the true temple.

John's message is that Christians must believe that Christ holds the key, and Christians must endure. Those who endure will have a crown (again, not the diadem of a king, but the wreath given to those who run the race and see it to its end). They will become pillars of the true temple. The conquerors will wear God's name (belong to God) and be citizens of God's new city. Calling that city the New Jerusalem again asserts the Christians' claim that the church is the true Israel.

The Letter to Laodicea (3:14-22)

Laodicea was one of the richest commercial cities in the world. It contained a famous medical school, a widely known clothing and wool industry, and a vast banking enterprise. Among its many medical products, Laodicea manufactured a highly regarded eye salve.

In the presence of this wealth, popular clothing industry, and remarkable eye medicine, John finds a church that has become spiritually poor, naked, and blind. Its affluence has closed its eyes to its own mediocrity. Neither hot nor cold, the Laodiceans' lukewarm religion has spoiled the church's savor.

John calls the Laodicean church *poor*, as he had called the church at Smyrna poor. He uses the same strong Greek word in both cases. Here, however, it does not refer to matters of wealth but to matters of the spirit. The Christians at Smyrna had almost no possessions at all; the Loadiceans possessed almost no faith at all. Christ calls the Laodicean church to recover its self-understanding, to see that it must define itself by what comes from Christ, not by what comes from the glamour of wealth that surrounds it. Christ's gold and garments and salve alone mark and heal the faithful.

Those who hear and respond to God's call will find themselves chastised. (Chastisement combines the two notions of punishment and being made pure.) But they will also find themselves surprisingly transformed into hosts; and Christ himself will come to dine with them. The Greek word translated *eat* may also be translated *to sup* and is the same word used in the phrase *the Lord's supper*. It means a long and intimate meal together.

The conquerors, again, are not those who wear crowns like the rulers of the secular world, but those who see the race through to the end. Their crowns connote victory after endurance, not royal power.

§ § § § § § §

The Message of Revelation 2:18–3:22

The letters written to the churches of Asia Minor are meant for all churches. The number seven is a symbolic number meaning *all* or *completeness*. The messages to them spoke both to the specific problems of each church and to the church in general.

The churches in the inland cities endured some trials in common with those on the coast. But they also faced some that were peculiar to themselves. To them John sent messages of both general and particular significance. Chief among those messages are the following:

§ Christians will face hard times and will also be severely tempted in good times.

§ God loves and will strengthen the faithful.

§ Not all danger arises from outside the church; distortions of belief and behavior can emerge from within, as well.

§ God knows the special circumstances of each church and Christian.

§ Immorality is not simply a matter of behavior. It can also stem from a lack of careful thought about the beliefs of the church.

§ Those who endure in faith will be rewarded by God.

§ Even those outside of the church can learn to worship in truth and find favor with God.

§ Christians should be watchful for the coming of God.

§ § § § § § §

Revelation 4–5

Introduction to These Chapters

In this part of the Book of Revelation, John shows his command of the apocalytpic books and images already in the Jewish tradition. Remember, the books we call the Old Testament were the Bible of the early church. John shows how, under the inspiration of the Spirit, those books and images gain newer and richer meanings. Images from Ezekiel and Daniel now bear witness to Christ.

John first describes the worship of God in heaven and then, at the heart of that celebration, introduces Christ. Chapter 4 focuses on God the Creator; Chapter 5 emphasizes Christ the Redeemer. Together, they set the stage for the series of judgments and promises that make up the remainder of the book.

This part has two sections:

 I. The Heavenly Praise of God (4:1-11)
II. The Scroll and the Lamb (5:1-14)

We will indicate at several points where the reader may look to find the Old Testament passages that became so important to John and his readers. Together they comprise a stunning repertoire of ideas and stories to nourish the hearts of the faithful. Comparing them to John's use of them shows the power of the Spirit to transform tradition into a vital message for the day.

The Praise of God (4:1-11)

John has just reported Christ's words to the church at

Laodicea: *If anyone hears my voice and opens the door, I will come in to him and eat with him, and he with me* (3:20).

Immediately, John looks to heaven and sees a door. The voice in his new vision calls him to the door. But he finds himself called, not to a meal, but to a view of *what must take place.* Similar visions may be found in Ezekiel 8:1-4 and 11:1-2. *The Spirit lifted me up between earth and heaven, and brought me in visions of God to Jerusalem* (Ezekiel 8:3)

In John's vision, he sees himself swept up by the Spirit and taken to the heavens where God dwells. While in heaven he sees God's throne. This royal image of God is very important to John, who wants always to contrast the apparent power of rulers on earth with the true power behind the scenes, hidden in heaven. He uses the word *throne* forty-seven times, many more than any other New Testament writer. He vividly reminds his readers that the earthly thrones—with which they had had much sad experience— are but pale imitations of the one true throne and the one true king who matters.

John's description of God (verse 3) resembles Ezekiel's (Ezekiel 1:26-28). The precious metals he mentions are not all known now. His language and the brilliant array of gems are meant to inspire awe and fear. But the rainbow, a sign of God's covenant with Noah, suffuses the entire scene with a gentle reminder of God's love and mercy.

Circling God's throne are twenty-four more thrones, occupied by elders who are wearing crowns and are dressed in white. The attire of the elders suggests that they are angels. The number twenty-four had rich symbolic significance: Twelve and its multiples were regarded as sacred and perfect numbers—there were twelve tribes and twelve disciples. Two times twelve (twenty-four) orders of priests are listed in Chronicles.

Both Jewish and Christian traditions often associate God's appearances with lightning and thunder; Exodus 19:16 and Ezekiel 1:13 are examples. Ezekiel also mentions torches of fire, although only John connects them with the seven spirits of God. Here again, the number seven symbolizes perfection and completeness. John, therefore, in verse 5 may mean "God's Spirit" or "the full Spirit of God."

In addition to the elders, four creatures surround the throne, one on each side. They are full of eyes—all-seeing—and have wings and voices. They gather together the gist of many ideas from ancient religious traditions. In particular, there is a teaching among the Jewish rabbis that there are four mighty creatures. The mightiest among the wild animals is the lion, the mightiest among the birds is the eagle, the mightiest among the domestic animals is the ox, but the mightiest of them all is the human being. The creatures described by John illustrate that the mightiest of the mighty, in their true nature, worship God.

The four creatures also illustrate how John combines features of his tradition in order to create the symbols he desires. The creatures see all (many eyes) and have great power (being made up of parts of the most powerful creatures), yet they all attain their true status only as they worship God. Nature, in all of its forms, is intended to worship.

The four creatures lead in praise of God. The creatures made up of powerful things worship the Creator of all things.

Around the throne, John sees what looks to him like a sea of clear glass. That image would have great effect in his day. Not having modern glass-making techniques, the ancients were unable to make clear glass. What they did produce was uneven and dark, often opaque. When John indicates clear glass, therefore, he suggests something marvelous to the eye, and of great splendor.

To the little churches in Asia Minor, this ceaseless worship illuminates the scene that is just behind the scenes of the history they are experiencing. No matter what appears to be the case on earth, God the Creator exists and knows all. The point of the universe is not power but worship. Do not bow before idols or earthly powers, but like heaven's awesome creatures, worship God.

The Scroll and the Lamb (5:1-14)

Chapter 4 began with a description of the place of the Creator and ended in worship. Chapter 5 describes the appearance of the Redeemer and concludes in worship of him.

John notes first of all a scroll with writing on its front and back, similar to what the prophet Ezekiel had seen years before (see Ezekiel 2:9). The scroll very likely contained God's plan of redemption for the world. The plan, initiated by Christ, awaits completion. It, and the faithful, still look forward to God's victory. Its being written on both sides symbolizes that it is complete and detailed.

Scrolls were sheets of papyrus joined end to end. The sheets were made from plants grown in Egypt. Papyrus pages had two dried pieces of the plant placed over one another, with the grain of one at right angles to the grain of the other.

Seven seals bind the scroll shut. They await opening. The opening will not only reveal God's plan, but will also set it in motion. But only one who is worthy has either the right or the power to open it.

John at first despairs of its being opened. An elder then points him toward one who is *the Lion of the tribe of Judah* (a phrase from Genesis 49:9 that depicts Israel as a great power) and is also the *root of David* (a phrase from Isaiah 11:1-10 pointing to a new king and deliverer of Israel).

John looks, only to see that now those two phrases have a new meaning. Instead of seeing a figure of great power and regal presence, he sees a lamb, one that has been slain. Christ, the slain and risen lamb, is the fulfillment of the hopes of the Jews (the Lion of Judah). Being of God, he is also not only from the line of David, but the root from which the line of David came. He is, in other words, the beginning and the end. Therefore, he is worthy to open the scrolls.

The choice of the word *lamb* for Christ is meant to be striking. The word is associated in the Roman tradition with weakness and in the Jewish tradition with the weak animal used for sacrifices. How the lamb runs counter to any image of power and prestige can be seen from the animals modern-day nations have chosen for their symbols (the Russian bear, the British lion, the American eagle). To show how misguided nations can be in their assessment of what matters most, John chooses to symbolize the Kingdom above all kingdoms with a lamb.

The lamb has seven horns and seven eyes. Horns are symbols of power and eyes symbolize vision. Together they present the lamb as having full power and all-seeing vision, attributes given otherwise only to God. Zechariah had spoken in a similar way (Zechariah 4:10). When each of those separate ideas combines with the rest—lion and lamb, power and knowledge (all-seeing), worth and sacrifice—they make up the meaning of the word *messiah*. Messiah is another name for Christ.

The lamb takes the scroll because it is worthy to do so. No other creature, not even those in heaven, is able to take the scroll. Not even heaven, then, has the perfection that God will eventually bring about through the lamb.

As the lamb takes the scroll, a hymn of praise tells why it is able to do so. First, it was slain to ransom people for God. Second, it has made of those people a kingdom and priests of God. Because it is worthy, the lamb receives praise, not only in heaven, but from the entire created order.

The word *ransom* in Greek means *to purchase*. God, in ransoming sinners, according to John, buys them back. Christians were purchased, however, not by a payment, but through the suffering of the lamb. Through God's own suffering, they now belong to God.

The slain lamb by whose blood Christians are ransomed reflects and recasts the Jewish ritual of Yom Kippur. Yom Kippur is a day of penitence among the Jews. It was celebrated with the sacrifice of animals on the altar. The sins of the people were symbolically affixed to the animals, one of which was offered at the altar, the other being sent into the wilderness, bearing with it the people's sins.

John uses that ritual to symbolize his understanding of Jesus. Jesus, God's lamb, died in order to rid people of their sins. In this case, however, God and not the people provided the sacrifice. God made forgiveness possible, bringing the people back.

In verse 9, John describes the elders and creatures at worship amid the incense which presents the prayers of the saints. The hymn of praise is, he says, a new song. A series of events is about to unfold which will lead to a new heaven and a new earth. They are introduced by a new song. For John, two themes intermingle. One, the church fulfills the promises of God from of old. Two, in some dramatic way, the old order is surpassed. Therefore, for him, the word *new* takes on great importance. When God brings in the new age completely, the faithful will have *new* names, they will dwell in the *new* Jerusalem, set within the scene of the *new* heaven and earth.

The newness began with the Lamb. One expression of that is the surprise that it is not the Lion of Judah, but the Lamb of God who inaugurates this fresh age. The motif of the lamb, in this setting, harkens back not only to the Passover festival, but to the story of Abraham and Isaac. Sacrificing lambs in the Temple was done occasionally as a memorial to Abraham's willingness to sacrifice Isaac, or, more accurately, to Isaac's willingness to be sacrificed. One traditional Jewish saying was that, through the merits of Isaac, God would raise the dead. One new age had begun with Isaac, an age that allowed the family of Abraham to grow and prosper. Now, through another sacrifice, one by God's lamb, another new age began.

§ § § § § § §

The Message of Revelation 4–5

John uses images and ideas from other apocalyptic books to interpret and explain his vision. Yet he also turns those images and ideas into a distinctively Christian message. The way he reworked those resources can be seen in his description of worship in heaven. What is the meaning of what he saw?

§ God is the center of all true worship.

§ The God seen by John is the same God of the Jewish tradition; the rainbow, symbol of God's covenant with Noah, shows that continuity.

§ No matter how things appear on earth, God dwells behind the scenes creating the example of true worship.

§ God has all power, and is working through events on earth, no matter how things seem.

§ God exalts the humble as servants who guide the unfolding of divine history.

§ Nothing in the present, on heaven or on earth, has yet achieved its perfection; only Christ has proven completely worthy to God.

§ § § § § § §

Revelation 6:1–8:5

Introduction to These Chapters

This part begins a series of chapters that describe God's judgment. The seven seals (6:1–8:5), the seven trumpets (8:6–11:19), and the seven bowls (15:1–16:21) all herald greater destruction. These sets of seven do not form a single continuous story line, going from beginning to end, but, more like preachers' illustrations, serve to emphasize a single point in increasingly intensive ways. Therefore, if they seem to conflict with one another in some details, they share in a larger agreement: God acts in history and will bring it to a just and imminent conclusion.

This part, dealing with the seven seals, falls into a pattern that John uses again with the trumpets and bowls. It divides the seven into a pattern of four, two, and one. An interlude usually falls between the middle two and the final item of the seven.

Here is an outline of Revelation 6:1–8:5.

 I. The First Four Seals (6:1-8)
 II. The Fifth and Sixth Seals (6:9-17)
III. God's People on Earth and in Heaven (7:1-17)
IV. The Seventh Seal (8:1-5)

Except for Chapter 7, these verses all describe types of destruction inflicted on the earth and its inhabitants. The wreckage is massive, but not total. It includes war, international strife, famine, pestilence, persecution, earthquakes, and cosmic signs. Predictions for such such widespread grief are not exclusive to Revelation in the

New Testament writings. They appear also in the Gospels. (See, for example, Matthew 24:2-9, 29; Mark 13:7-9, 24-25; Luke 21:9-12, 25-26.)

The view of God here is much like that in the first chapter of Genesis. There, God had but to speak, and what was said came to pass. *And God said, "Let there be light"; and there was light* (Genesis 1:3). Here, God's words about the future are in a scroll. The scroll has only to be opened, and what God has written will come to pass.

It is also well to note here that John relies heavily on the Exodus experience of the Jews in order to interpret how God creates the events of these and the following chapters of Revelation. In the Exodus story, Pharaoh refused to obey the messages Moses brought from God. God, in response, turned the natural order against Pharaoh as punishment. Water turned to blood and pestilence stalked the land. In Revelation, it is not the land of Egypt alone, but the entire globe that is affected. And, as we shall see, with each set of seven judgments the natural disasters become more intense.

The First Four Seals (6:1-8)

These four seals bring forth the famous "four horsemen of the Apocalypse," each laying waste to the world in his own assigned way.

The lamb opens the seals; the plan of God unfolds through the work of the lamb. As each seal is opened, one of the four creatures who surround God's throne summons forth a horseman. The first horseman inflicts war. The second unleashes the warring hatred of men upon each other. The third horseman, dressed in black, brings famine. The scales he carries indicate that grain will have to be carefully weighed and distributed. A denarius was about one day's wage; the grain it would buy was about one day's food—enough for one person, but not enough for a family.

The creature orders the horseman of famine not to

harm oil and wine. One Jewish tradition taught that the coming of the messiah would be preceded by a time of great evil but abundant wine.

The fourth horseman, death, is followed by Hades—the place where the dead dwell to await resurrection. Together they affect one-fourth of the earth. Ezekiel also associates God's judgment with death by sword, famine, pestilence, and wild beasts (see Ezekiel 14:21).

The Fifth and Sixth Seals (6:9-17)

The scene shifts to heaven (verses 9-11) and then to the earth and sky (verses 12-17).

The fifth seal reveals the souls of the martyrs who, dwelling under the altar, rest also under the perpetual gaze of God. These martyrs—people killed because of their faith in God—cry out for justice. In Jewish law, all court cases were civil cases—one person accusing, another defending. If one party were ruled right, the other, of necessity, was wrong. Human events had judged the martyrs wrong. They now plead with God to set the record straight. In response to their plea, they are given white robes and are told to rest. The Greek word translated *rest* here means to tarry and find refreshment.

In verse 10, God is called *Lord*. This translates a Greek term for one who is the master of slaves. But here the meaning is enriched. The master is not a tyrant, but is one who is holy and true.

The dour estimate that yet more Christians would be killed reminded Revelation's early readers that their tribulation had not yet ended. The notion that the number of martyrs had a limit and that God would soon intervene, however, held out hope for those who endured.

All of the images of verses 12-17 were familiar to John's readers. They occurred in biblical and other religious books, and would have been a way of saying that the end was near and that God's kingdom was coming about.

Some books in the library John consulted are Isaiah (13:9-22); Ezekiel (32:7; 38:19); Hosea (10:8); Joel (2:10, 30-31); and Amos (8:8). John paints a scene filled with cosmic and earthly upheaval, when even God's enemies recognize God's acts and power.

John's images here are very similar to those in Matthew 24:29-31, where Jesus speaks of the sky being darkened, the stars falling, and the heavens being shaken.

God's People on Earth and in Heaven (7:1-17)

This chapter functions as an interlude and has three parts: verses 1-8, 9-12, and 13-17.

Verses 1-8 address the worries of those faithful ones who remain on earth: How will they fare in the wake of so much destruction? God's seal is set upon them. The seal identifies them to the world as God's people. It also assures God's people that God knows they are the chosen ones. The number who are sealed is symbolic. It is the multiple of the square of twelve (a symbol for Israel) and the number ten (the symbol for perfection). It therefore stands for the true Israel, which is the church.

God's people are called *servants*. The word in Greek does not refer to servants in the modern sense— hired helpers. It means *slaves*. The word emphasizes utter devotion. However, like the word *Lord*, it also reverses some of the meanings attributed to it in its culture. As the Lord God is not a tyrant, but holy and true, so the slaves are not servile, but faithful and loving priests.

The *four winds* of verse 1, in Jewish writings, cause destruction similar to the horsemen (see Psalm 18:10 and Zechariah 6:5). The word refers to storm winds that bring disaster and devastation.

The listing of the tribes of Israel in verses 4-8 illustrates the symbolic use of numbers among both Jews and Christians. The names appear in at least twenty different orders throughout the Bible. Further, the names are not always the same. In this, the tribes resemble the lists of disciples, which also appear in different orders and with some differences in names. In each case, however, care is taken to keep the number at twelve—a number representing completeness or totality.

In Revelation, John lists *every tribe of the sons of Israel* this way:

Judah
Reuben
Gad
Asher
Naphtali
Manasseh
Simeon
Levi
Issachar
Zebulun
Joseph
Benjamin

Numbers 1:14-44 lists the tribes this way:

Reuben
Simeon
Gad
Judah
Issachar
Zebulun
Joseph
Manasseh
Benjamin
Dan
Asher
Naphtali

Both the order and the contents differ (Levi replaces Dan) in the list in Revelation. John's list resembles that used by Ezekiel (Ezekiel 48:30-35). Ezekiel was an important part of John's library.

The list used by John may have been arranged according to the matriarchs rather than the patriarchs of

Israel. The order shows six sons of Leah, two of Rachel, two of Rachel's handmaid, and two of Leah's handmaid. That would fit well with the pattern in Revelation of viewing the faithful on earth in maternal terms. The church is the bride; the symbol of the faithful is a woman (see Chapter 12)—even those who are within the church but lead it astray may be women, as, for example, Jezebel in Thyatira.

John's attention turns in verse 8 from earth to heaven. A vast wave of worship rolls through the heavens, moving through all who are there. A great multitude, beyond number and representing all nations, praises God. Each wears a white robe; in this case, a gown for celebration similar to the one given the prodigal son on his return to his father's home. Palm branches are symbols of victory—appropriate for the hands of those whom John calls conquerors.

In verse 13, an elder tells John that the members of the great multitude are those who have endured the tribulation. From the vantage point of the end of history, one can see that those who endure in the struggle of faith against evil, in truth populate God's court. Those of the world cannot see that, for it is a hidden truth—one that John now reveals for the sake of encouraging his readers.

The elder speaks in the form of a poem. The poem sums up the fondest hopes of the Jews, whose teachings continued to feed the minds and spirits of Christians. Among the Old Testament verses echoing through this poem are Psalm 121:6; Isaiah 25:8 and 49:10; and Ezekiel 34:23.

The elder describes God's care for those who endure: shelter, no more hunger or thirst, living waters, and, above all, a time when grief will finally be over.

Verse 15 transplants a beautiful Old Testament idea into a new setting. The martyrs are before God's throne and *serve him day and night*. In return, God *will shelter them with his presence*. That phrase may also be understood, *His*

Shekinah shall abide upon them. The *Shekinah* means the presence of God, and occasionally abides upon God's people on earth—in the tabernacle, in the Temple, in Jerusalem, or among the chosen people elsewhere. Here it carries the meaning of shelter and protection.

The lamb will *guide* the believers as a shepherd. Shepherds lead with strength and from familiarity with their flocks. It is an important reversal of the world's standards, where lambs are meek. The church, meek by wordly standards, will be led with strength.

The Seventh Seal (8:1-5)

The last seal opens to a deep and pregnant silence. The scene is still heaven, but the angels, elders, and creatures have been stilled so that the prayers of the saints may rise like incense to the center of God's attention. A Jewish teaching had it that God silences the angels by day in order to hear the prayers of Israel and show it kindness.

The tranquility is not permanent but preparatory. Against the background of charged silence, a fresh statement of God's judgment is being readied. Seven angels with seven trumpets appear. They will deliver the next series of judgments.

Verse 2 speaks of the seven angels who stand before God. While the number seven has symbolic meaning, it had another set of connections in the mind of Jews and of the early Jewish Christians. That connection was to the seven angels of the Presence. The angels, and the meanings of their names, continued to figure into the unfolding story of the Jewish people. The angels are: Uriel (fire of God), Raphael (God has healed), Raguel (friend of God), Michael (he who is like God), Sariel (prince of God), Gabriel (God is my strength), and Remiel (possibly thunder of God).

In several places in the Old Testament, angels are mentioned as either leading the people or driving away their enemies. Exodus 23:20, 2 Kings 19:35, and 2 Chronicles 32:21 are examples. The tradition gradually developed into the belief that God's angels divided into military legions, of which these seven were the heads. The persistence of the belief can be seen in Matthew 26:53 in which Jesus speaks of calling upon *legions of angels.*

An overture precedes those judgments, however. The prayers of the saints have been mingled with incense, rising from a censer held in an angel's hand. The censer, perhaps symbolically carrying the fragrance of God's mercy, then is hurled to the earth. Earth and sky both shudder in the wake of the concussion, with thunder, lightning, and earthquakes. The censer of sweet fragrance and violent concussion vividly reminds John's readers that on the other side of God's mercy lies God's judgment.

§ § § § § § §

The Message of Revelation 6:1–8:5

John sees a stark example of divine judgment. The judgment is not wicked revenge, but justice, a repayment for sin and wickedness. John's vision of the seven seals is told to the seven churches to reassure them that the flow of history is in God's hands and that God is just. He also wants them to understand that:

§ The judgment human beings experience they often inflict upon themselves—war, famine, and hardship: the affliction of the four horsemen.

§ Even the power of kings and other rulers is held at God's permission.

§ Ultimately, nothing goes beyond the ability of God to control.

§ Christians who suffer death for their beliefs will be especially honored by God.

§ God knows and listens carefully to all faithful believers.

§ § § § § § §

Revelation 8:6–11:19

Introduction to These Chapters

This part of the Book of Revelation divides into five parts:

I. The First Four Trumpets (8:6-13)
II. The Fifth and Sixth Trumpets (9:1-21)
III. The Small Scroll (10:1-11)
IV. The Two Martyrs (11:1-14)
V. The Seventh Trumpet (11:15-19)

Again John deals with a set of seven by dividing it into smaller groups of four, two, and one (the first six divide into four and two). And again, he places a long interlude between the sixth and seventh.

The trumpets, like the seals before them, unleash terrible havoc upon the earth. In the Jewish tradition, trumpets were associated with battle (see Zephaniah 1:15-16), with the approach of the *Day of the* LORD (Joel 2:1), and with worship. They were associated especially with the worship on the tenth day prior to the Day of Atonement: the Day of Judgment. Together, the trumpets announce that history and nature belong to God, who judges it, redeems it, and now readies it for entry into the new age.

This part also shows with clarity John's familiarity with and appreciation for Old Testament ideas and Scriptures. He uses them this time in a form of writing that was very common in his time, a form called *typology*. Typology means using familiar types of images and events to quickly communicate new messages and their urgency. One of the most familiar to John's readers was the story of the Exodus and the events leading up to it.

In the Exodus, God delivered the Jews from bondage in Egypt. Pharaoh, king of Egypt, had kept the Jews as slaves. Pharaoh's refusal to release the slaves led to several traumatic events. God created plagues and other afflictions to persuade Pharaoh to let the people go.

Eventually Pharoah submitted. The Jews went free. The story of that release was repeated by the Jews in special ceremonies every year. For them, God became forever identified as the one who freed them from slavery. And the plagues remained symbols of the extent to which God was able to go in order to set them free.

Because of the power of the Exodus story, John repeats fragments of its themes, and when he does, his readers know enough to fill in the blanks. They know John is talking about the acts carried out by God in preparation for the delivering of the people. Those events remind people that that is the type of thing God does to set the stage for the next, more compelling act—hence, the word *typology*. Among the ingredients from the Exodus story, John will use sudden darkness, locusts, bloodied water, famine, and death.

The First Four Trumpets (8:6-13)

Each of the first four trumpets affects one-third of the earth. The punishments, while battering, are not total. The breadth of the wreckage, coming from earth and heaven, sharply contrasts the range of God's power with that of earthly kings. They may rule their plots of land; God rules the universe. The church is reminded in this way to keep its faith focused on God. Those who knew the Exodus story would recognize the afflictions (fire, drought, bitter water, sudden darkness); they occurred also when God sought to break the Jews free from their bondage in Egypt.

The first trumpet picks up themes from Exodus. The second uses themes from Jeremiah (51:25), where God's judgment casts down a mountain. The third trumpet draws its themes from Isaiah 14:12-20, a potent reminder that those who attempt to rise like the stars and rival God will be cast down. *Wormwood* is an aromatic plant, also known as *absinthe*; it has a bitter taste. An early form of this word eventually became, in English, *vermouth*. The falling of the star and its trail of destruction are recorded in the English word *disaster*, *aster* being the Latin word for star. A disaster is a fallen star.

The fourth trumpet sounds echoes of Exodus again (Exodus 10:21 and following), in which God sends a plague of darkness. The section ends with the mournful cry of an eagle: More is yet to come. There will be three woes, one for each of the remaining trumpets.

The Fifth and Sixth Trumpets (9:1-21)

At the sound of the fifth trumpet a star falls. The star may be a symbol for an angel or a reference, as in Chapters 1 and 2, to a part of the church (or other earthly inhabitants) gone bad. The result is that a shaft is opened and locusts pour out. Both the Exodus story and Joel 1–2 provide John with references for this description. The effect of this trumpet is felt not only by nature, but by humans as well.

An *abyss* is a place that harbors evil spirits.

The locusts have human faces, possibly meaning that John wishes to describe the evil that humans perpetrate upon each other. As they swarm, it becomes obvious who their leader is: Apollyon. John links another name with that of Apollyon in order to make one striking point. That name is Abaddon. *Abaddon* means, in Hebrew, *destruction*, and, at times, *Hades* or *death*. Translated into Greek, *Abaddon* becomes *Apollyon*, which means *perdition* or *destruction*. But Apollyon also sounds much like the name of the Greek god Apollo, whom the

Romans worshiped and the emperor Domitian claimed to incarnate. John has created a very telling play on words. Domitian, the Greek and Roman god he worshiped (Apollo), and those who followed all add up to perdition and destruction. John carries the play on words even further, for the symbol of Apollo's cult was the locust.

In Chapters 12–14 of Revelation, John will again take aim at Apollo. There he will take a familiar story about Apollo's birth and turn it into a Christian parable. In the ancient story, the dragon Python waited near Leto, Apollo's mother, for Apollo to be born. John turns the tale upside down by regarding Apollo as the destroyer and Christ as the child to be born.

In 7:1 John described four angels at the four corners of the earth. In 9:13, as the second woe, God looses four other angels, this time from the river Euphrates. That river divided the Roman Empire from the Parthian lands. Twice the Parthians had defeated the Roman armies. The Parthians had invented a clever and effective strategy for battle. They rode horses directly at their enemies. Then, abrubtly, they turned around, riding away from the enemy, firing arrows at them while escaping. The famous "Parthian shots" left enemy foot soldiers wounded and helpless.

The fierce Parthian soldiers raised fear in the minds of the Roman people. They feared this great army of the north. John's Jewish readers were also familiar with the idea of great armies from the north. Isaiah (14:31), Jeremiah (1:13; 6:1, 22; 10:22), and Ezekiel (26:7; 38:6) had all spoken of them. They were actually and symbolically frightening.

John builds upon Roman fears and Jewish prophecies, then, to construct a vision of uncompromising terror. Troops and beasts combine to slay a third of humankind. John heightens the terror by using all of the symbols of God's most terrifying judgments and of Hell: fire, smoke, sulphur, plagues, beasts, and serpents.

In 9:20, John tells the purpose of the devastation. It is not the vicious strike of the claw at helpless victims; it is the hammer blow at the manacles that chain people to idolatry. In spite of all, John shows, most prefer their chains.

The Small Scroll (10:1-11)

John begins with a vision that draws upon Daniel 10:4 and following: an angel surrounded with symbols that assured the readers of its divine origin. An important message is to come. The angel strides land and sea; a sign, perhaps, that the result of his message embraces the entire globe. A small scroll nests in his hand.

The angel shouts. The heavens answer with a message that John describes as *thunder*. John seeks to write what the thunders have said, but a heavenly voice stops him, ordering him to seal up what he has heard. John's retelling of that incident serves as a warning to us that even students of Revelation do not know all that was said and seen. Certainly they do not know enough to warrant making predictions; much, even in the unveiling of Revelation, remains sealed away from us.

The Greek word translated *seal up* literally means *to keep hidden*. A seal, in the ancient world, not only bound a message shut; it also showed the identity of the person who sealed and sent it. We still know that form of seal from products that bear the "seal of approval" of agencies that set standards, or from the presidential seal on letters. God wants parts of John's knowledge sealed off, kept hidden, and for the reader to know it has been God's doing.

The angel then announces that, at the last trumpet, God's mystery should be fulfilled. The *prophets* referred to in verse 7 are probably New Testament martyrs; it is to them that God promises fulfillment.

John is told to take the scroll from the angel's hand and to eat it. He does, and finds it, as the heavenly voice had said, sweet to the mouth and bitter to the stomach. That combination of sweet and bitter leads to an order to John and through him to the church—they must prophesy. The gospel, sweet on their tongues, may yet for a while lead to the bitterness of martyrdom.

Verses 9-10 are very close to Ezekiel 3:1-3. There, Ezekiel is told to eat a scroll and then go to speak to the house of Israel. Ezekiel says that he took the scroll, *Then I ate it; and it was in my mouth as sweet as honey.* John eats a scroll and then is ordered to *again prophesy about many people and nations and tongues and kings.* While the scroll turned bitter in John's stomach, only the words spoken by Ezekiel turned bitter, as they announced God's judgment of Israel. Jeremiah also describes his experience of receiving God's word with the analogy. And again, there is the combination of sweetness and bitterness. Jeremiah writes, *Thy words were found, and I ate them, and thy words became to me a joy and the delight of my heart.* But he goes on to say, *Thou has filled me with indignation* (Jeremiah 15:16-17).

The reception of God's word, then, in John's tradition, brings both pleasure and discomfort. That may mean either that the experience of hearing God's word is warm and positive, but the message to this imperfect world will of necessity bring grief and bitterness; or it may have nothing to do with the experience, and simply be a symbolic way of speaking about what God has to say: God's word, spoken or written, holds the promise of mercy but speaks realistically about the duress the believer must face.

The relationship between eating and gaining knowledge is very ancient. The Eden story in the Old Testament spoke of a tree of the knowledge of good and evil, whose fruit imparted spiritual knowledge.

The Two Martyrs (11:1-14)
John uses many Christian symbols now to create a

Christian parable. The Temple in Jerusalem separated the faithful from all others. Now, in John's time, faith itself separates Christians from all others. Measuring the Temple (a scene whose original type is found in Ezekiel 40–48) now means taking the measure of true believers. The length of time, *forty-two months*, uses important numbers in Jewish apocalyptic thought. They have their origin in Daniel 9:24-27 and 12:7. They have, as their meaning, the last years of human history.

John's reference to the *temple of God* in verse 1 places a Jewish symbol in a Christian setting. The Jewish Temple in Jerusalem clearly separated the Jews from the Gentiles. In Herod's Temple, stone walls kept the Gentiles from entering the inner areas which the Jews occupied. In some periods, the outer court was called the *Court of Gentiles*. That may be the *court outside the temple* John has in mind. John gives that symbol, familiar to his readers, a new meaning. The Temple, altar, and worshipers are now the Christian community. The outer court and the holy city represent the area that will be given over to the rule of the forces of evil. His message is that, for the brief time to come, all but the faithful will be under the sway of evil. That does not mean that the faithful will be protected from physical harm. The Temple in Jerusalem had been destroyed by the Romans, and many faithful Jews had experienced great misery. So now, during the reign of evil, the Christians (the true Temple) would feel the press of evil. They needed to know that, wherever they went and whatever they endured, from God's point of view, they were the inner circle of the Temple, the holy ones of God. God had taken their measure.

The length of time, *forty-two months*, is mentioned in verse 2. Verse 3 uses the figure 1,260 days, which is forty-two months of thirty days apiece. The number occurs also in 12:6; 13:5; and in 12:14, where it is a period described as three years and a half, or, literally, *a time, times, and half a time*. All of these refer to the same thing.

(A *time* = 1 year; *times* = 2 years; a *half a time* = 1/2 year. The sum is 3-1/2 years, or forty-two months.) The origins of the number are in Daniel 7:25 and 12:7. There the expression is *time, times, and half a time*. It also appears in Daniel 9:27 as a *week of years*, which is seven years. Daniel divides that week in half to arrive at three and a half years. Again, it equals forty-two months.

The symbolism is important for understanding John. Daniel is a very important part of John's library. Daniel's verses refer to a time when Antiochus ruled Syria. He badly persecuted the Jews. In 168 B.C. he placed an image of the Greek god Zeus on the altar of the Temple in Jerusalem. Daniel speaks of that as the *desecration*, which he expected to last three and a half years. It had taken Antiochus three and a half years to commit the act. When the next three and a half were complete, Daniel expected God to unveil a new age and to bring about the resurrection of the faithful.

The Jews did recover the Temple in 165 B.C.—an event which they celebrate to this day in the feast of Hanukkah. The new age did not come. But, in Jewish and Christian thought, the three and a half years (forty-two months) following the desecration carried much meaning. It spoke symbolically of the need to endure and of the nearnesss of God's great and final act of deliverance.

The *two witnesses* may be the two churches, Smyrna and Philadelphia. Both were called blameless in the letters sent to them. Jewish tradition had prepared the notion of two witnesses at the end time, although the characters changed; sometimes they were Enoch and Elijah, sometimes Moses and Elijah. Zechariah had written of two olive trees (4:3), a symbolic reference to the king and high priest of his day. John combines the two witnesses with two lampstands of Revelation 1:20 to show that he means now to use the traditional symbols for two witnesses to refer this time to the two churches.

Jewish tradition surrounds powerful divine speech with vivid natural images such as lightning, thunder, and smoke. John shows the importance of the two witnesses by showing how they speak with the power of cosmic collapse, driving rain, and menacing plagues. Through them the God of the cosmos addresses humankind.

Sodom and *Egypt* (verse 8) were two places of unrivaled sin. To the Jews, they symbolized the earthly city in its most wanton rebellion against God. The *beast* from the *pit* (verse 7) had, from Daniel on (see Daniel 7:2-21 and 11:31-39), symbolized unbridled evil.

John expects death for the witnesses, who lie in the streets *three and a half days*; again a symbolic reference to Daniel and the time of tribulation. John also illustrates, through the witnesses, that he did not preach a gospel of success. Those who kept the faith did not ultimately romance the world or its economies into acceptance. Nor does the natural order cooperate with Christians to guarantee that their kind of goodness will find its natural reward in wealth and glee. The world's inner logic is spun by minds captivated by evil. The blameless may express their power, but the slant of the world is against them.

The witnesses have *finished their testimony* (verse 7). The word *finished* here means not only that the testimony has ended but that it has been completed, has achieved its aim. The servants have said what needed saying.

It is God, not the world, who summons the witnesses to life and then to their heavenly home. All of nature reacts—an earthquake followed by the toppling of buildings and the death of 7,000. John ends this grim parable with the reminder that it is only the second woe. Another remains.

The Seventh Trumpet (11:15-19)

The story of the trumpets continues. The two witnesses were a parable within the story, but more now must be said.

The seventh trumpet leads, not to the end as one expects, but to worship that forecasts the end. The raising of the two witnesses had begun, but was not completed, making the kingdom of the world become the Kingdom of Christ. The process of rewarding the faithful had begun, which is more than a note of hope to those of John's readers who still faced martyrdom.

The seventh trumpet (verse 15) points attention back to the ceaseless worship that takes place in heaven. So confident are those in heaven of God's victory on earth, that they sing as though it were already accomplished. The twenty-four elders say a poem that shows how Psalms 2:2 and 22:28 will ultimately find their fulfillment. From the perspective of the end of history, even though the nations rage, God's *wrath came, and the time for the dead to be judged, for rewarding thy servants, the prophets and saints.* It has not happened on earth, but it is so certain that, in heaven, it is possible to worship as though it had already happened.

The ark of the covenant is described in 1 Kings 8:1-11. The earthly ark had served to witness to the covenant between God and the people of Israel. John transplants the ark to heaven, where it witnesses to the covenant between God and the Christian church. That covenant can be seen in the song in verse 18: *rewarding thy servants* and *destroying the destroyers of the earth.* Nebuchadnezzar, ruler of Babylon, had destroyed the Temple in 586 B.C. The ark had been lost. Once it had been lost, the thought gradually came to pass that the ark ought not be found. In Jeremiah 3:16-18 the prophet describes all of Jerusalem as the throne of the Lord. Previously, the ark had dwelt in the holiest part of the Temple. In Jeremiah's belief, all of Jerusalem would become the holy place. In a sense, the entire city becomes an ark, the place of God's presence. In fact, a legend existed that Jeremiah had hidden the ark on the same mountain which Moses had climbed. Clearly, the people were no longer to think of God's presence as limited to the actual physical ark.

John takes the process one step further. The ark is in heaven. It is now the pure symbol of the presence of God.

In this chapter, then, two objects grow through important changes. They begin as objects, then become symbols for a spiritual idea on earth, and then become symbols of something even more spiritual in heaven. The physical ark, which locates God's presence and power in a very small space, expands to become a symbolic way of speaking about a much larger place (Jerusalem), and finally describes God's full presence in heaven. The same holds for the role of the temple. First it stood for the actual building where the Jews worshiped. Then it expanded in John's usage to refer to the Christian church. Then, in verse 19, it refers to the place in heaven where the elders and martyrs perpetually worship God.

§ § § § § § §

The Message of Revelation 8:6–11:19

The seven trumpets repeat in many ways the events of the seven seals. John repeats and expands the seven seals for emphasis. He wants to inspire the confidence of believers in God. He uses many familiar and potent symbols to do that.

What meaning does John wish his early readers to find as they read his book?

§ God liberates the faithful from bondage.

§ The God who liberates them is the same God who liberated the people of Israel from Egypt.

§ The dangers to Christians are often those of loyalty to or worship of something other than the true God.

§ Not everything has been revealed, and therefore not everything can be known. Although history is in God's hands, beware of those who think they know all they need in order to tell the hour and the day, or to make all of the details plain.

§ God remains a mystery; no one knows precisely what God will do. But God's justice can be relied upon.

§ Faithful witnesses will not always find the world friendly; but God will not forget them.

§ § § § § § §

Revelation 12–14

Introduction to These Chapters

To describe this vision, John uses a spectacular parable.
The characters in the parable—a dragon, two beasts, a
woman, and a child—change meanings from time to time.
But they combine to tell a story of gross events, malicious
motives, and sometimes frightening peril. The parable
also features the stuff of great drama: dramatic rescues,
armed conflict, betrayal, and the collapse of a great
power.

John doesn't mean this, however, as simply a dramatic
presentation. His parable reduces nearly the whole of
religious history into a story about beasts and people. He
intends that his readers shall find themselves in the story;
that they will know where they are in it, and which
nations and rulers are being referred to.

The parable has the following outline:

   I. The Dragon and the Woman (12:1-6)
  II. Satan Is Cast Out of Heaven (12:7-12)
 III. The Dragon Pursues the Woman (12:13-17)
 IV. The Dragon's Servant: The Beast (13:1-10)
  V. A Second Beast Worships the First (13:11-18)
 VI. The Martyrs Worship in Heaven (14:1-7)
VII. The Fate of the Unfaithful (14:8-13)
VIII. Judgments Begin (14:14-20)

This parable summarizes John's moment in history: evil
on the rampage, with its followers in high worship of it.
The church is under duress. But, backstage, God has
already begun changing the scenery for the final act.

Babylon, the nation that plundered the Temple centuries earlier, is the central symbol of evil and rebellion. It stands for Rome.

The Dragon and the Woman (12:1-6)

John sees a *portent* in the sky. A portent may also be translated as *sign* or *wonder*. It carries a meaning or message often from the future to the present and therefore is filled with hints and intimations of what may be yet to come. A portent is not a photograph of the past or future. It is symbolic, and its meaning lies in what it points to. In this case, the portent points to God's word behind the scenes—past, present, and future. But it needs interpretation, some of which John will provide. Much of its meaning, however, would have been clearer to those in his culture who knew its stories and symbols.

Dragons appear under several names as symbols of evil in Jewish writings (see, for example, Job 26:13; Psalm 74:13-14; Isaiah 27:1 and 51:9). The Old Testament also uses the image of the pregnant woman to refer to the faithful. Isaiah describes Israel as *a woman with child, who writhes and cries out in her pangs* (Isaiah 26:17; see also Micah 4:10).

The woman symbolizes the people of God, from the Jews through the church. It is important that the reader keep in mind that she is not simply a symbol for Mary, the mother of Jesus, but also of the people of Israel, who, through Jesus, gave birth to the church. She is also, at times, a symbol of the church, which gives birth to the faithful. She is called a *portent*, which translates a Greek word meaning *sign*; in this case she is a sign of God's intent to bring forth a faithful people. God's work through history with the Jews, and now through the church, shows God's intent. Her pregnancy heralds the bringing forth of the messiah but also of the church.

The dragon, like the evil dragons in many ancient stories, has seven heads. *Horns* are symbols of strength and power. The dragon is the ancient powerful agent of evil: Satan. He awaits the child, who is the symbol of God's promise to bring forth a faithful people. The stage, therefore, is set for the cosmic struggle between God and evil, with the action focused upon the faithful whom God loves.

The woman gives birth. God saves the child. The woman, now no longer a symbol of Israel, but of the church, has a safe place prepared for her for 1,260 days—a symbolic number for a time of great trial. And again, the equivalent of a time, times, and half a time—three and a half years.

The parable compresses a great amount of time into a brief moment. The birth of the child becomes immediately the moment of his being taken up into heaven; the birth of Jesus turns instantly into his resurrection. The Messiah, once born, becomes the crucified and risen lamb.

Satan Is Cast From Heaven (12:7-12)

The parable looks to the cosmic battle of good against evil. The church is reminded that it is embroiled in more than just a local struggle. An angry Satan rages in its midst.

Satan and *devil* each mean *accuser*; the first in Hebrew, the second in Greek. *Satan* first referred to an angel who watched people on God's behalf, reporting their faults and sins to God. By the time of the New Testament, *Satan* and *devil* referred to one who tempts people into trouble and, if they cannot be tempted, slanders them. He is the arch deceiver. In John 13:2, the devil deceives Judas Iscariot into betraying Jesus.

The battle in heaven was not a new thought in either the Jewish tradition or those that surrounded it. Many parables existed to express how evil, in spite of God's power and love, got its reign upon the earth. John offers no explanation for how evil originated in heaven. But he does testify, at the end of Revelation, that even the present heaven will be replaced with a new one, one from which all sources of evil will be expunged.

The Dragon Pursues the Woman (12:13-17)

By now, in the parable, the woman has become the church. John's view of her is kaleidoscopic, changing somewhat depending upon the light he wishes to set upon the church's present distress. The dragon pursues the woman. The Christians of his time, suffering under the persecution of Domitian, now know that Domitian is the dragon, the devil's own instrument—possibly the devil himself. Domitian had regarded himself as the incarnation of Apollo, a pagan god.

Given wings, the woman flees to safety, as, possibly, very many Christians had gone, for the present, to be with God. The event again reaches into the riches of the Exodus story for some of its meaning. The dragon spews water after the fleeing woman. The earth swallows the water, making a safe way for her. The church is saved, just as the people of Israel had been saved during the Exodus when God parted the waters, allowing them to move to safety over dry ground.

To describe the time of her safety and of the duress of the church on earth, John uses the symbol of *a time, and times, and half a time*. It refers to Daniel 7:25, the time of duress prior to God's final act. It equals 1,260 days (a number we have seen before): *a time* = 1 year; *times* = 2 years; and *a half a time* = 6 months. Together they equal 1,260 days.

Some additional information about Chapter 12 may be useful. John, through this parable, was able to make even the pagan religions pay homage to his God. His parable about the pregnant woman converts several pagan stories into a witness to God and the church.

Many stories in the religions surrounding Asia Minor tell about a monster waiting to devour children who are about to be born. One of them, and the most pertinent, concerns Apollo. According to the story, Leto, Apollo's mother, had to escape from the serpent Python. Python knew that he was fated to be slain by Leto's son, so he sought to devour the son as soon as he was born. Poseidon, the sea god, rescued Leto, and took her to safety on the island of Delos, which was visible from Patmos. John, of course, takes that pagan story and makes it witness to his God. The woman becomes the Jewish nation, then Mary, then the church. The beast becomes Satan. The child is Christ.

See Revelation 9:11 for John's attitude toward Apollo. Note that John uses that name to refer to Apollo as the destroyer. Cleverly, John was preparing the way for his parable. Apollo may be a god in Greek myth, but John knows him as the destroyer. Christ is the true savior.

The Dragon's Servant: the Beast (13:1-10)

A beast rises from the mysterious depths of the sea, as the terrifying beasts had in Daniel 7:2-7. Like Satan, this beast has seven heads and ten horns, making it obvious that the new evil reflects the old. The crowns it wears are not victors' wreaths, which are the crowns for the faithful who endure to the end. They are crowns of royalty. This beast claims vast earthly power. It very likely represents the arrogant and willful power of Rome.

In Daniel, the leopard, bear, and lion represent different nations (see Daniel 7). Here, one beast combines all features; it presumes enormous earthly power. The dragon gives power to this beast. The beast, then, incarnates cosmic evil in the Roman empire. Seven heads may refer to the seven principal Roman emperors. There had been eleven emperors, but three had together barely lasted a year, and were scarcely of sufficient stature to count in the dimensions of evil that John had in mind. The wounded one may refer to Nero, who, though dead, was widely rumored to be returning, possibly to initiate yet another siege of insane butchery.

The beast's power lasts 42 months (again, the accumulation of a year, two years, and half a year). As in Daniel (7:21), the beast wars upon the saints. John alludes to Jeremiah 15:2, to direct the Christians' response: Accept prison; do not kill; endure.

A Second Beast Worships the First (13:11-18)

This beast represents the imperial priesthood, those who enforced and celebrated the worship of Rome and its emperor. This beast, to some a tempting parody of the church, appears like a lamb. But its voice gives it away; it speaks with the dragon's voice. Possibly luring Christians with the promise that worshiping it was compatible with worshiping Christ, the Roman cult actually spoke evil's party line.

In the parable, the priests make an image of the beast and, by magic, make it speak. John thereby reduces to its silly essence any religion that invents the divinity of a nation (or creature or ideology) and then pretends to give it voice. All along it is the power of the state manipulating the charade. What John reveals is that, while the state may not know it, it itself is being manipulated by evil.

The *mark of the beast* may be the sign given those who worshiped Caesar. Obviously, Christians would not worship Caesar, and thus, rather than being marked by him were marked for trouble.

The beast's number, 666, may have been clear to the early church. We have lost the key to understanding it. One suggestion is that, if we use the numerical values Greeks gave their letters, the Greek name for Jesus equals 888. The number seven, or a series of number sevens (777) means perfection. Hence, Jesus is more than perfect (as eight is more than seven), while the beast, whose number is 666, is less than Jesus and also less than perfect. That means that, in spite of its pretenses and marvels, the beast is flawed and so is any worship of it.

The number of the beast has fascinated students of the Bible for centuries. Not only the Greeks, but other ancient peoples also matched numerical values to the letters of their alphabets. Some scholars have sought letters of the Hebrew alphabet, for example, to match the numbers 666. The problem for all has been to find a name from the early Christian era that has letters that equal that number.

One popular, but complicated, solution has been to say that the number means "Nero Caesar." If one takes that name in Latin, then puts it in the form of the Greek language, and then substitutes Hebrew letters for the Greek letters, and then converts them to their equivalents in numbers, one gets 666. That result has its attractions, partly because in some ancient manuscripts of the Bible the number is not 666 but 616—and that is what one gets if one bypasses the Greek language and translates the Latin directly into Hebrew.

The fear in John's time that Nero would rise from the dead to resume his persecution of Christians has made Nero Caesar a popular choice with some interpreters. Some in that time also believed that Domitian was simply a new version of Nero. The number, then, applied to him.

Others have generalized the number 666. They believe that it does not stand for any individual at all, but for all of humankind, or for that portion of humankind that is evil. In that case, John would be saying that all who are not faithful bear the mark of evil.

Because of the uncertainty of our knowledge of the number's meaning, some interpreters have thought that it refers to someone who might arise after John's time. They have invented ingenious solutions which attempt to show that the number refers to other historical figures, usually figures regarded by the interpreters as completely evil. Among those who have been selected have been popes, political leaders, economic leaders, and the spokespersons for other religions. During World War II, some Christians took Hitler to be the beast with the number 666.

For the most part, however, students of the Bible resist trying to find contemporary figures to match the number of the beast. John was dealing with his own time, and the number can be made sense of in his own setting.

The deeper truth behind the number, however, can be applied to John's time and to all time. The conflict between good and evil, between 888 and 666, seems a permanent feature of history. It will take many forms, but underneath it will be the same struggle. And in its midst, Christians will have to endure and conquer.

The Martyrs Worship in Heaven (14:1-7)

The parable continues by showing, against the backdrop of the beast's feverish attempts to elicit worship, the pure and true worship offered in heaven. The contrast continues: these worshipers have God's name, not the beast's, on their foreheads.

Mount Zion had great symbolic power for Jews and Christians as a place of deliverance. Psalm 2:6 and Joel 2:32 both make reference to it.

John's reference to Mount Zion has more than passing significance, then. The two beasts of Chapter 13 arise, one from the earth and one from the sea. Both occupy low-lying places of the terrain. The Lamb stands upon the mountain. Geographically, John displays the dominance of the Lamb over the beasts.

But his use of Mount Zion gives his point more power. Mountains were associated with great formative events in both Jewish and Christian traditions. Moses received the Law on Mount Sinai. Jesus faced temptation on a mountain, was transfigured on a mountain, and spoke one of his most memorable sermons on a mountain. Clearly, they were sacred places.

But John refers to a specific mountain, Mount Zion. Zion was originally the name for the crest of a hill in the southeast part of Jerusalem. The name grew in significance as the result of several events. When the Temple was built and the ark of the covenant was transfered there, the name *Zion* tended to include the Temple. God was said to dwell on the Mount of Zion. Pilgrims came yearly to "mount to Zion" to worship.

The belief built up among the Jews that, when God decided to glorify the faithful, it would be done on that mountain. In some Scriptures, Zion even came to mean the heavenly Jerusalem.

Psalm 2:5-9 illustrates how many Jews and Christians came to think of Mount Zion's place in God's final plans.

Then he [God] will speak to them in his wrath,
  and terrify them in his fury, saying,
"I have set my king
  on Zion, my holy hill."
I will tell the decree of the Lord:
He said to me, "You are my son,
  today I have begotten you.
Ask of me, and I shall make of the nations
  your heritage, and the ends of the earth
  your possession.
You shall break them with a rod of iron,
  and dash them into pieces like
  a potter's vessel."

Mount Zion was the place where God's appointed ruler was expected to show forth God's power, and where the nations, however they arrayed themselves militarily, would crumble under the might of God's chosen one.

One hundred and forty-four thousand martyrs worship in heaven. Not only are they martyrs, but they are male and chaste. Why only males? This may be the explanation. In Chapter 7, John showed the 144,000 recruited from every tribe. Psalm 2, his point of reference, has to do with arraying troops for battle against the kings of the earth. The 144,000 may be all male because they are following the regulations of Deuteronomy for Holy War (see Deuteronomy 20 and 23:9-10).

War in Moses' time and in John's vision is no purely secular or national affair. Many believed the outcomes depended upon the wills of the gods and their grand schemes for history, and on the careful obedience of the faithful to even the minutest religious ritual. Religious ceremonies prepared armies for war and soldiers were commanded to remain ceremonially pure. That meant abstaining from sexual relationships. During the time of ceremonial cleansing, prior to battle, a soldier who became impure had to remain outside the camp for the day, and could return only after day's end, following bathing.

That ceremonial purity is, for John, also a symbol of moral purity. He sees the Lamb prepared for battle on the mountain. The enemies surround the land and sea below. Nothing less than total purity is required of those who join the Lamb. Again, John draws from his tradition, intensifies it, and makes it transparent to a newer meaning.

The worship scene concludes with an announcement by an angel. The announcement spreads over heaven and earth. It calls for repentence and true worship. The time of judgment has come. The parable, at this moment, reaches beyond events of the past and present, moving to the end of history to show how things will appear from there.

The Fate of the Unfaithful (14:8-13)

Three more messages pour from heaven upon the earth. First, Babylon (Rome) is as good as fallen. Second, the beast's worshipers will face eternal torment. Third, the faithful will find rest and blessedness.

The third angel says, *If anyone worships the beast and its image . . . he also shall drink the wine of God's wrath.* Its followers, hearing the warning, have a chance to stop. If not, the empire and its cult will suffer the fate of Sodom and Gomorrah: fire and brimstone.

In verse 12, John halts the parable in order to interpret for his readers. It is a call to the saints to endure. The divine promise of rest and peace will follow.

Judgments Begin (14:14-20)

Having portrayed the contrast between earth and heaven, John now extends the parable to include God's judgment on Rome.

John uses the language of Joel 3:9-14. Judgment is depicted in the quick and deadly cut of the scythe and the torturous deliberateness of the wine press. The Old Testament uses *harvest* and *vintage* often as symbols of divine judgment. *One like a son of man* is also a traditional symbol for the time of judgment. Both Daniel and Jesus spoke of the *Son of man* who would come to deliver God's people, bringing God's justice with him.

Verses 14-16 follow from verse 13. The harvest of the faithful is ready. The angel frees and gathers in the faithful from the earth.

Verses 17-20 conclude the parable by showing a harvest of the sinful, not in the folds of heaven, but on the plates of the winepress.

The complete parable, therefore, directed to the faithful in the churches of Asia Minor, puts the suffering of their moment in time in the setting of a much larger story. They live a chapter in the history of the cosmos. What God began early with the Jews has taken this course of events. The tensions increase between God and all of earth's incarnations of evil. From the ground level one sees evil all around. From God's perspective, the limitations of evil are visible. So is the steady press of God toward the fulfillment of history. God will care for the church as he cared for the woman. The message of the parable to those little churches is clear: Endure, for God's victory is assured.

§ § § § § § §

The Message of Revelation 12–14

John often speaks to the church in what seem to us to be alarming ways. The parable of the woman, the dragon, and the beasts is an example. He uses the items in his parables in sometimes changing ways, like the shifting color schemes of a kaleidoscope. But always he controls his stories for the purpose of making his central point: God rules history.

He also makes these points through the parable:

§ When we look simply at immediate events, we may not see the fullness of God's plan as it unfolds.

§ The prophetic books of the Bible and the great story of the Exodus help us see the larger picture of God's work.

§ The church, in remaining faithful, will often experience great stress.

§ Christians will always face the temptation of worshiping the ideals and idols of their nations.

§ God may not be apparent, but God is at work among us.

§ The power of evil is great, and must not be underestimated.

§ The rule of evil is limited.

§ God's blessing is on the faithful.

§ § § § § § §

Revelation 15–16

Introduction to These Chapters

In this part, John again combines scenes of worship in heaven with scenes of destruction on earth. And again, in the telling of the story, Babylon symbolizes Rome, and, by extension, all that Rome has polluted on earth.

John shows his command of typology by putting the story in the form of the Exodus. Typology is a way of telling a story by putting it in the form of a more familiar type of story, or of taking events that are familiar, and using events of that type in a new story. Typologies help readers see the significance of an event by reminding them of other similar events.

In this case, John's story contains many of the ingredients that make the Exodus so memorable. It includes plagues, a sea around which the faithful may gather safely (as the Israelites did about the Red Sea), references to Moses (who led the Israelites through the Red Sea), and a reminder of the tent of witness where the stone tablets bearing the Ten Commandments were kept during the years the people of Israel traveled in the wilderness.

John's story has four sections:
I. The Song of the Conquerors (15:1-4)
II. Presentation of the Bowls of Wrath (15:5-8)
II. Four Bowls of Natural Disaster (16:1-9)
V. Three Bowls of Warfare (16:10-21)

The word translated *wrath* comes from a root meaning violent movement, something boiling up. The English word *wrath*, closely related to the word *writhe*, means to twist in torment. In John's story, then, God's wrath is the final boiling over of judgment, and the unrepentant are shown in torment.

Two additional points need to be made. First, John seems to have come close to ending his story many times. If one were to total up the destruction delivered upon the earth thus far, the scourges and their aftermaths, surely little would remain for further destruction. If nothing else, the delicate membrane of the earth's ecology would have torn from the excessive pestilence and violence.

It is good for us to remember that John is not telling a single story. He has a single theme, but several stories, each illustrating the theme with greater power. His strategy is not to write a chronological history, but rather to write about the meaning of history. And that can be done best by making his point in several ways. As far as he is concerned, his readers must see God's justice as the final force and the driving force in history. And they must believe that it rises above and overreaches any other apparent power in their day. His successive images, stories, and teachings accumulate a weight of persuasiveness that no single part could do by itself.

Second, the brutality of John's images often offends the minds of those who have set their hearts upon a God of love. John's heart was set upon that same God. His use of images almost always comes from a careful use of the Old Testament. He chose the images that his readers would recognize. He used them because he wished to show that he spoke and wrote with the authority of the ancient belief, and to remind his people in sharp ways that his God was no fly-by-night deity. This was the God about whom the ancients had spoken. None other.

In a time of great duress, the images of power were needed to speak to power. But, to John's credit, he never let sheer malice get in the way of justice. And, to the end, he assumed that God's heart was open to those who would worship God in spirit and truth.

The Song of the Conquerors (15:1-4)

John again turns to the ceaseless worship that takes place in heaven. His attention is on wonders. Wonders are signs of God's activity.

John's reference to plagues hearkens back to the Exodus story, a reminder again of God's mighty acts to deliver the Hebrew people. The word *plague* means *to strike*—an indication of their quickness and violence. They are to complete the work of God's wrath.

The bowls, or cups, of God's wrath are familiar and potent symbols from the Old Testament (see, for example, Isaiah 51:17-22).

The sea of glass mingled with fire is John's attempt to find words to describe what really appeared: a scene of transparent brilliance, featuring those who survived the tortures brought on by the beast. Those who survived, the *conquerors*, sing a song that is filled with important symbols and references. Their song, the song of Moses, ties the plagues and the deliverance of the faithful to one and the same God who delivered the Jews from bondage. It is the lamb's song as well, marking a deliverance that is not only a natural event, but a cosmic event as well. Further, it is an event brought about by the crucifixion. Ultimately, it is God's self-sacrifice, more than any other thing, that brings meaning to history and its closure.

The song is written in the style of Hebrew poetry, with the second lines in each set of two either repeating or augmenting the thoughts of the first. All of the ideas are drawn from Old Testament sources. Again, John shows how the Old Testament, the Bible of the early church, can be viewed in a fresh way in order to present its witness to the crucified and resurrected Lord

Presentation of the Bowls (15:5-8)

The Ten Commandments are the witness to God's covenant with the people. From the time of Moses, keeping the commandments has been the standard demanded of the Jews. Jesus also taught that those who seek eternal life must not break the commandments (see Luke 10:25-28). The commandments were kept in the tent of witness while the Jews roamed the wilderness outside of the Promised Land. In heaven, the temple is the tent of witness. There, the commandments continue to witness to God's faithfulness and righteousness.

The seven angels step from the tent; only God remains within. Smoke pours forth. Smoke was often a sign of the presence of God (Exodus 40:35; Isaiah 6:4; Ezekiel 44:4).

The bowls, or cups, which are handed to the angels are the same as those that held the prayers of the saints in Revelation 5:8. Possibly the imminent plagues carried within the bowls are God's answer to the prayers of the saints.

Piece by piece, John is collecting the significant ideas from the Exodus story, magnifying them through the lens of the end of history, and showing how they may now speak of God's final acts in history. From here on through the rest of his book, John is almost totally replacing the scenery of everyday history with that of the most significant events in Jewish history. With Moses, the plagues, and other items depicted in this section, all of his readers would be awaiting, with confidence, the final stroke of victory for God and God's justice.

Four Bowls of Natural Disaster (16:1-9)

The first four bowls have to do with the havoc that can be wreaked when nature's most vile moods are loosed.

They contrast with the last three, which spread over nature's violence the debris of human animosities. Together they sum up symbolically the potential for carnage invested in the moods of the Creation. But in John's hands, they do not point backward alone, to sins committed and now to be paid for. They point forward to final acts of God, with justice given and blessedness deserved.

In John's previous stories of judgment, damage had been done only to parts of the earth. In these final judgments, the damage extends much further. The contents of these disasters, however, resemble those of the four trumpets. The difference is in the degree of intensity and in the increased range of devastation. For example, in this series of plagues, foul sores afflict not just a fraction of the people, but all who worship the beast.

The *voice from the temple* belongs to God. The plagues strike quickly, like those inflicted upon Egypt. John makes strong parallels with the Exodus: The sores reflect those that distressed the Egyptians (see Exodus 9:10) as does the alarming transformation of water into blood (Exodus 7:19).

The *angel of the waters*, like those mentioned earlier who controlled the four winds, has control of a region on God's behalf. He declares the justice of turning the waters into blood as punishment upon those who had so recently spilt the blood of the saints.

The *voice of the altar* may be that of the angel who came from the altar in Revelation 14:18.

Three Bowls of Warfare (16:10-21)

The fifth angel pours wrath upon the *beast*, Rome, itself. No longer will punishment affect only its followers. The focus draws increasingly upon those who lead the rebellion against God. Darkness covers all, as it had covered Egypt in Exodus 10:21. The sixth angel dries up the river Euphrates. The Euphrates formed a natural barrier that protected the Romans from their dreaded enemies, the Parthians. The dried river was an invitation to attack.

This time, not only the Parthians gather for the attack. The dried river clears a place for the gathering of all kings and armies for the final battle.

The dragon, beast, and false prophet (the second beast that worshiped the first), sprinkle flattery over the other rulers, enticing them to join together for the battle. The flattery is venomous. The frogs, symbols of pestilence, also reflect Exodus (8:1-7).

Armageddon is a Greek translation of a Hebrew word meaning *the mountains of Megiddo*. Megiddo was the site of a famous battle (Judges 5:19-20), although the city itself does not sit upon a hill. It symbolizes the place of battle, where the kings of the earth gather to do battle with God.

The seventh angel pours from his bowl. It is the sign for God to announce the end. Accompanying the divine voice are the terrible signs and sounds of divine action—lightning, thunder, and earthquakes. In the prophetic tradition with which John was familiar, earthquakes often accompanied the final acts of God. (See, for example, Isaiah 13:13; Haggai 2:6; Zechariah 14:4-5.)

The earthquake breaks apart the cities of the kings. Babylon, symbolizing Rome and all of its evil, crumbles. John uses all of his tradition's signs to make clear what he means: The end has come. God's justice is established.

The removing of the mountain, also a traditional sign of God's deliverance, draws from Zechariah 14:10. The plague of hail first occurs in Exodus 9:18, and reappears in Isaiah 28:2 and Ezekiel 38:22. John's careful selection of events and images from the Old Testament reinforces his claims by tying them to several familiar passages dealing with justice and the end of the world. In this case, the prophetic texts overlie the Exodus story—a powerful combination speaking uninterruptedly of deliverance.

§ § § § § § §

The Message of Revelation 15–16

John again describes his vision by using symbols from the Book of Exodus. He uses versions of the plagues once visited upon the Pharaoh to interpret the meaning of God's action in history. As the plagues spelled disaster for the Egyptians, they spelled hope for the Israelites who were in bondage. Similarly, the plagues now become symbols to speak of the disaster that awaits those who perpetrate evil, and to bring hope to those who wait faithfully for God. And, as in the time of the Exodus where the Pharaoh lined up his troops for warfare against God's people, here all of the kings line up their troops for a final battle against God.

For John, this is no simple re-enactment of an old story. He has his own message to send, one that speaks through the old story, but in greater, and graver, terms. What is that message?

§ God is active, not passive, in history.

§ The same God who delivered the Jews from Egypt is at work to save the faithful from the forces of evil.

§ The tent of witness, important for God's original covenant with the people of Israel, remains important; the commandments remain in force.

§ God is the ruler of nature as well as of the human world.

§ God's justice has to do with all of the nations, not simply with those who have known and worshiped God.

§ History is a limited process, and will have an end. Beyond history, and larger than it, is the kingdom of God.

§ § § § § § §

PART
TEN **Revelation 17–18**

Introduction to These Chapters

Revelation 17:1–18:24 and 19:1–20:15 tell two stories, but they are meant to stand side by side. In the first story, John tells of an evil woman who rides upon the beast of Chapters 13–14. She is given the name of *Babylon*. Babylon, to all who knew the Old Testament (and the Greek Old Testament was the Bible of the early Christian Church), symbolized great evil. Babylon had pummeled and destroyed Israel, exporting her riches, breaking up her families, and razing her place of worship. It was while in exile following that brutal attack that the psalmist had written, *By the waters of Babylon, there we sat down and wept, when we remembered Zion* (Psalm 137).

But John wants his readers to know that, in his telling of the story, Babylon is used as a symbol. It is Rome he has in mind. The beast he describes offers us some decisive clues in that direction. The seven heads of the beast, he explains, are seven hills—the seven famous hills upon which Rome sat. The seven heads also are the seven kings. Rome had had more than seven kings, but, as we shall see, the mathematics of Revelation are not meant to be arithmetic so much as symbolic. As such, they not only denote the rulers of Rome; they have a message to send about them.

The second story (19:1–20:15) works in contrasts. The evil woman (Rome) is compared to the good woman, the church, the bride of Christ.

Here is an outline of these chapters.

The Harlot and the Beast (17:1-6)

The Old Testament frequently calls the worship of other gods "harlotry." Isaiah 23:16 calls the nation of Tyre a harlot because it does not worship the God of Israel. Nahum 3:4 speaks in the same way about Nineveh. Those who seek intimate relationships with persons other than their own spouses step outside the marriage covenant. Similarly, those who worship other gods seek to share the deepest relationship of their lives with one who is not the God of the true covenant.

John's reference to *many waters* is explained later in verse 15. The many waters stand for people of many nations and tongues. The harlot, therefore, is a city that draws its nourishment and strength from many nations. The nations, in turn, have become dependent upon her largesse. She has seduced them into dependency upon her, as a harlot seduces one to become dependent upon her for meeting one's needs, and as a false god entices persons to his worship through the promise of boons and satisfactions.

John is taken into the wilderness to get a better perspective on the idolatrous city. In the Exodus, the desert is where the Jews went to receive a truer perspective on God.

John switches the picture to suit his message. He is not offering snapshots, but symbols that convey a message. He places the woman on the beast. She wears all that the world regards as beautiful—although in its accumulation it presents the gaudy more than the beautiful. The beast is scarlet, the color of royalty and of Rome. Its seven heads are the seven hills of Rome; its horns are the seven kings.

Roman harlots wore their names on their headbands. This harlot wears the name of Babylon, the great symbol of evil to all who knew the Old Testament. The reference to the blood of the martyrs would have left no doubt in the minds of John's readers as to the identity of the harlot: Obviously it is Rome.

The Harlot and the Beast Explained (17:7-14)

In order to explain his vision, John shifts his perspective again. The woman and the beast each so exemplify evil that John can trade their attributes back and forth between them.

The beast is explained first. Rumor had it that Nero, who had persecuted Christians in Rome, and who had died in A.D. 68, was coming back to life. To some people, Domitian, the emperor during the time John wrote, seemed already very much like a second Nero. The more evil changes, the more it is the same old thing.

The seven heads are Rome's seven hills, the seat of power and imperial control—and of impurity, as John saw it. Shifting interpretations again, John also suggests that the beast's heads are the kings, the principal rulers of Rome. Two points of view, then, combine to make one point: Roman power and leadership are integrally evil, and slated to become worse.

The eighth head, according to John, is one of the seven. There had been, in fact, eleven kings of Rome including Domitian. But three of them (Galba, Otho, and Vitallius) together had barely served a year. They could hardly be considered as leaders. The eighth king, then, might refer to Nero, whose death some believed was not final.

However, seven is also a symbolic number for completeness, and John may simply have been pointing to seven kings as a way of saying that the earthly rule of the world was coming to its completion. If that is the case, then, to keep the symbolism straight, the eighth king would have to be one of the original seven. In that case, John may mean that he expects Nero to reappear as an emperor.

The symbolism of the ten horns comes from Daniel 7:7. They stand for power, and, on the beast, they indicate the beast's power over the heads of every nation. They will all join the beast in the battle against the lamb of God.

The Fate of the Harlot (17:15-18)

In John's new angle of vision, the woman stands for Rome, and the beast and the ten horns refer to all of the other leaders and nations she has misled. The harlot lives by her seduction of the others.

John foresees that the woman's "lovers" will tire of her and organize against her. The beast may represent the vast power of evil that influences all of the evil empires. John sees, however, that even such enormous evil can be made to serve God's ends.

The Lament of Heaven (18:1-8)

This section combines three threads. One is the song of doom, which is characteristic of many Old Testament prophets. In this case the song is written in the traditional form of Hebrew prayer, poetry, and prophecy. The second is the connection of the symbol of Babylon to Rome. The third is John's pastoral concern for his early readers.

The words spoken by the angel in verses 2-3 and by the other voice from heaven in verses 4-8 follow a form typical of Hebrew poetry. The form can be found in most of the psalms and many sections of the prophetic writings. In that form, the same thought is presented in two or more lines, but is expressed in different words.

For example, verse 2 repeats in three different ways the same idea of how Babylon has fallen:

It has become a dwelling place of demons,
  a haunt of every foul spirit,
  a haunt of every foul and hateful bird.

Again in verse 8 the second line repeats and expands the idea of the first:

So shall her plagues come in a single day,
  pestilence and mourning and famine.

This poetic form helped give the listener a second chance to hear a major idea and also offered the poet and preacher a chance to repeat and strengthen a point.

First, an angel speaks, using the phrases and predictions of the Old Testament prophetic tradition. These songs of doom spoke with great truth to John's early readers. They originally spoke of the fall of other great cities like Tyre and Nineveh. Now they speak of the ruination of the city of Rome and of its pernicious influence. The first words spoken by the angel come from the lips of Isaiah (Isaiah 21:9). Similar images of the desolation of great cities (including Babylon) haunt other passages of Isaiah (13:19 and Chapter 34), as well as Jeremiah (50:35-38) and Ezekiel (26:1-6).

Like Babylon, Rome has not only befouled itself, it has lured others to its nest. John likens their cooperation with Rome to a sexual seduction, for which generous payment has been made.

Pastoral concerns now speak through the story. John describes another voice in verse 4, possibly the voice of Christ. The voice calls the faithful out of the city, as God had called Abraham out of Haran and Moses out of Egypt. In each case, the evil vests in cities, and deliverance calls the faithful out into the wilderness. John is telling this stark story for their sake.

The voice then speaks to the ranks of heaven (verses 6-9) to order the final fall of Babylon. Again John illustrates the force of his story by using powerful Old

Testament symbols: pestilence, plague, famine, and fire. The true Exodus, of which the first from Egypt was only a pale original, is about to take place.

The Lament of the Earth (18:9-19)

The scene shifts abruptly into the future, to describe how kings and merchants and shippers will react to the fall of their economic "lover." They form a chorus of unlikely, fearful, and selfish mourners.

Again, the lament is written in the poetic form. It can be seen clearly in verse 14:

The fruit for which thy soul longed
  has gone from thee,
and all thy dainties and thy splendor
  are lost to thee, never to be found again!

The kings of the world weep and stand off in fear. While they want Babylon's (Rome's) business, they don't want her torment. They are able to recognize the devastation not as a natural disaster, but as a judgment.

The merchants mourn as well. But they do not mourn for the city and its people; they mourn for the loss of a good market for their wares. They, too, stand off, wary of having to share Rome's torment.

The shipmasters and their crews also mourn the fatal closing of their finest market. John chooses here phrases with strong echoes of Ezekiel (see Ezekiel 26:16-17 and 27:30—the latter should be compared especially with Revelation 18:19). John's language is the traditional language associated with the fall of great cities.

The shipmasters' lament should conclude at the end of verse 19, starting with a recognition of the great city and ending suddenly with a parallel recognition of how quickly it was laid waste.

This lament shows how very far-reaching were the economic lines that held the world to Rome, and how lavishly Rome used the goods of the world. Verse 11 speaks of the cargo bought by Rome. *Cargo* was any load of merchandise, no matter how it was carried. Rome, of course, received hers over both land and sea. We get clues from the lament that tell us how much of the world supplied Rome's desires.

Linen came from India. Silk may have come from China through India. Scented woods came from North Africa, and were used to make expensive furniture. Ivory may have come from India or Africa. Cinnamon came from China. Spices often came from Mesopotamia. Incense, myrrh, and frankincense came from Arabia. Grains came from Egypt. Horses came from Armenia.

Not to be missed here is the trade of slaves, "human souls," side by side with the dainties that sweetened the tongues of the wealthy. That small word, *slave*, refers to a vast source of Rome's economic strength. Slaves did not count as persons, and could be dealt with as an owner chose. Successful persons could be expected to have at least a dozen slaves to serve them in their households, and could have hundreds more to work their fields. In fact, slaves became commodities for trade, much as linens and precious metals had.

When John, in other parts of Revelation, calls Christians *servants*, the word he uses is the word for *slave*. Slaves belonged completely to their masters; Christians belong completely to Christ. No competing loyalties are allowed.

The Angel With the Stone (18:20-24)

Although verses 17-19 are written in the past tense, John moves here quickly to the present tense. He urges heaven and earth to rejoice over the fall of Babylon and to acknowledge that the fall was God's judgment on that city. The Greek word translated *judgment* refers to an act of justice, not of vengeance. John wishes always to make clear that Babylon and her accomplices got no more than they deserved.

John, still describing his vision, tells of an angel hurling a stone into the sea. The stone's fall symbolizes Babylon's fall. It recaptures a most striking Old Testament image. Jeremiah (51:63-64), upon writing about the evil of Babylon, gives his friend the following instructions:

When you finish reading this book, bind a stone to it, and cast it into the midst of the Euphrates, and say, "Thus shall Babylon sink, to rise no more, because of the evil I am bringing upon her."

The angel's song also follows the pattern of Hebrew poetry. This time the repeated refrain *shall be . . . no more* tolls the lament like a funeral bell. John speaks of the angel in the present tense, but it is clear that the events described are yet to come. The laments of kings, merchants, and shipmasters, told for dramatic purposes as a report of what the angel said in the past, are, in fact, part of a great prediction of the future.

Each of the angel's grim pronouncements about the fate and abandonment of Babylon strikes up a familiar and potent theme from the Old Testament (Jeremiah 25:10; Ezekiel 26:21). John uses here the darkest part of his tradition to assure his readers that the evil done to the faithful will not go unnoticed by God.

§ § § § § § §

The Message of Revelation 17–18

This part of Revelation reveals John's sense of the global web of evil. No nation is in it alone; each builds upon and prospers from the production of others—evil or good. Rome was not the first city to use such a web to capture others, and would not be the last. Babylon was a similar city, and had become in Jewish thought the ranking symbol of the evil city. Similarly, the prophetic protest against Babylon became the most striking condemnation of the evil city.

John's message, then, makes brilliant use of the old and familiar symbols to describe a new and unprecedented power. In the process, he also makes clear that the evil that nations do does not necessarily unite them. Bound together in order to feed from Babylon's (Rome's) prosperity, the nations disengage quickly when she faces grief.

What is the message of John in this light?

§ Even the amassed powers of nations cannot equal the power of God.

§ The economic motives that bring nations and people together are not sufficient to keep them together when times are hard; for that, a deeper bond, one of faith, is necessary.

§ The symbols and teachings of the church provide the decisive clues to the meaning of events; Scriptures that are in the form of predictions can often help us understand and interpret our present time.

§ All worldly power, however awesome it seems in the present, is temporary. Nations rise and fall; only God endures.

§ God acts in history and will speak the final word.

§ § § § § § §

Revelation 19

Introduction to This Chapter

In this part John moves in increasingly wider circles.
From the judgment upon Babylon he moves to the
judgment upon the beast and false witness, then to the
nations they and the woman deluded, including the kings
who had lamented the fall of Babylon. It leads to a
decisive, but not yet final, battle.

This part communicates its message through a series of
rich contrasts. John contrasts the groom (Christ) to the
beast, the purity of the bride (the church and the
church's martyrs) to the gaudy sinfulness of the harlot,
the sanctity of the New Jerusalem with the squalor and
spoilage of the degraded city, Babylon.

The point of these verses has as much to do with God
as with the church and its martyrs. Ultimately, the issue
to be decided is not one between the church and the
forces of evil, but between God and the forces of evil.
What is at stake for John is the conviction that the world
is God's. That is why, so very often in his book, he
pauses in his depictions of the turmoil on earth to
describe the acts of worship taking place in heaven. The
heavenly beings see clearly the God who is the true king
and ruler of the universe. It is God who is being belittled
by those on earth who claim power for their own, and
especially by those who organize cults to worship other
gods, and even themselves. John's book vindicates God's
ownership. To the opening hymn of Genesis, *In the
beginning, God* . . . he now wishes to add the final verse:

"In the end, God."

Here is an outline of this chapter.

I. Voices Rise From Heaven (19:1-5)
II. The Marriage Supper of the Lamb (19:6-10)
III. The Great Battle (19:11-21)

Voices Rise From Heaven (19:1-5)

God is praised, not so much for the victory over evil as for the exercise of justice. Although the previous chapter ended in the future tense, this one presumes the strife is over. The martyrs for God have had their deaths avenged.

The song makes clear that God's actions are not arbitrary. The harlot has corrupted the earth, God's creation. She has also exacted the ultimate price from the martyrs. God's actions appear appropriate to those who suffered through the difficult days.

It does seem less than Christian to rejoice in the maiming of others, no matter how evil they have been. John does not sidestep the issue. In his view, justice relates closely to mercy; in fact, it is one aspect of it. Those who remained faithful have earned the right to the reward, the other side of which is the justice meted out to those who opted for less honorable paths. It is important to bear in mind throughout the final chapters that John does not see punishment as a contradiction to God's nature. Christians throughout the centuries, however, have disputed John's view of how that justice is, and will be, expressed. None have disagreed with him that justice matters greatly to God.

The Marriage Supper of the Lamb (19:6-10)

John has just described the worship in heaven, celebrated because of the demise of the harlot. He now shows that the defeat of the harlot was not the true point of the celebration. It is the introduction to a marriage feast.

The marriage feast shows how intimately Christ and the church are related. This is a bold image, but one for which the way had been prepared. Some of the most winsome passages of the prophets describe God as the groom and the people of faith as the bride. The notion lay deep in the soils of Jewish culture and belief. Some of those who used it most tellingly are Isaiah (54:6), Ezekiel (16:8), Hosea (2:14), Matthew (22:2), John (3:29), and Paul (2 Corinthians 11:2). John sharpens the image. Christ is the groom; the church is the bride.

The bride's dress is the pure linen of the righteous. That clothing is meant to contrast with the lurid colors of the harlot.

The angel orders John to write (reminding us, again, that some things he has seen he has been ordered not to write). The words he writes are a beatitude: *Blessed are those who are invited to the marriage supper of the Lamb.* The marriage feast is the full and final celebration in the life of the church. For the early Christians, the weekly gathering for the Lord's Supper was an anticipation of that final celebration. John was reminding them that they took the bread and wine of that supper *until he comes again.*

John once more seeks to worship the angel who guides him. The angel refuses to be worshiped. John is told that even angels are simply fellow servants of God. The equality of all before God matters more than any distinction of rank between creatures.

The *testimony* of Jesus refers to the way Jesus witnessed throughout his life, his teaching, and his death. A *witness* is one who has seen a fact or a truth, and who testifies to it. Jesus' testimony, then, is what he said and showed about the truth. All true prophecy reflects Jesus' own testimony.

The Great Battle (19:11-21)

John interrupts the wedding scene. His vision shifts from the tumultuous preparations for the wedding to the heavens and a startling scene unfolding there. A rider, who is called *Faithful and True*, appears, sitting upon a great white horse. The rider is Christ. But he comes prepared for a battle, not for a marriage feast. The threat of the final showdown has loomed large throughout the book. Now, as a preface to the wedding, the battle is to be completed.

The white linen of his troops signifies their purity. His robe is dipped in blood—a sign of his martyrs' deaths and of his own crucifixion. The sword of the mouth is a symbol for speaking the truth (which cuts life into the true and the untrue, the just and the unjust). *Eyes of flame* is probably a metaphor for how it feels to be seen by one who can, as the saying puts it, "look right through you."

The crowns this time are diadems, the marks of royalty. They contrast with the crowns given the martyrs, which were wreaths given to those who endured through the race, like victors in athletic contests. Christ wears many diadems—a contrast to those of the beast and its rider, which were allotted only one to a head.

Christ's name is both the *Word of God* (by which all believers knew him) and a name *which no one knows but himself*. His depths are not fathomed by human reason, even the reasoning of the faithful. He is also *King of kings and Lord of lords*. Arrayed against all of the kings and lords of the earth for a battle, he only is the true King and Lord. The sword of his mouth, then, is the power of the word of truth, which he wields with the accuracy and power of a true king.

Verses 1-16 have set the stage for the battle. An angel precedes the battle with a forecast of the result. It comes ominously, not as a threat to the nations opposing Christ, but as an invitation to predatory birds to prepare themselves for a feast.

The battle ends instantly. John does not describe its tactics and strategies or its calculated maneuvers. In the ultimate contest between God and the powers of evil, there can be no contest. God's power alone can sway the future. Even the accumulated armaments and troops of the world's greatest nations are less than puny in comparison. This, in fact, is the ultimate contrast in John's book. The faithful versus the followers of pagan religions, the church versus the world, the bride versus the harlot, and finally, the King versus the kings. No matter how strenuous and discouraging the church found its life to be, reading Revelation assured it that none could stand up to Christ.

The battle ends quickly. The beast is captured, along with the false prophet who led others to worship it. The birds respond to the invitation and feast on the carnage. Again John works in contrasts—the grizzly feast of the birds of prey and the joyful wedding feast of the faithful in Christ.

Brimstone means *burning stone*. Some believe it also has reference to the odor of sulphurous fumes.

§ § § § § § §

The Message of Revelation 19

This chapter brings the struggle between heaven and earth to the threshold of its conclusion. The battle has been fought and won. There remains, however, the final disposing of the "enemy" and the happy conclusion for the faithful.

In moving to this point, John has gone through three different kinds of events: worship, wedding preparations, and warfare. Although they each would normally be considered quite differently from the others, John has, in fact, a few similar messages he wishes to communicate through those events.

§ God, and nothing and no one else, is the subject of John's book and of the lives of Christians.

§ God desires to relate closely to those who are faithful.

§ The image that best defines how God wishes the church to relate to him is that of the bride. For the faithful, the relationship is to be as celebratory as a wedding and as heartfelt and longlasting as a covenant between lovers.

§ God contains all of the powers admired on earth, but in the greatest degree possible. All earthly pretenders to power are trivial compared to God.

§ Justice will determine the fate of those who serve God and of those who oppose God's purposes.

§ § § § § § §

Revelation 20

Introduction to This Chapter

In this part of Revelation John tells about the final stages through which God subdues evil. Although the time span he discusses lasts for more than a thousand years, he condenses it into four brief sections. Further, he uses each of those sections to capsulize one significant event.

This part also continues the story line from Chapter 19. The defeat of the beast and its priest/prophet brings Satan, death, and Hades to their final destruction.

The four sections of this part are:

I. The Temporary Binding of Satan (20:1-3)
II. The First Resurrection (20:4-6)
III. Satan's Last Act (20:7-10)
IV. The Death of Death and Hades (20:11-15)

This chapter has led to many differences among Christians. Those differences stem from their understanding of the meaning and the timing of the millenium.

In this chapter, John sees a vision of an angel capturing and binding up Satan. Satan is then thrown into a pit for 1,000 years (*millenium* means *one thousand*; hence the millenium refers to a period of 1,000 years). The millenium is connected with the resurrection of the martyrs. According to verse 4, the martyrs come to life again to be with Christ during those 1,000 years. The remainder of the faithful dead and others come to life only after that.

The question that divides many Christians has to do with the time when Christ will rule on earth. Will he return, raise the Christians from the dead, and rule on earth with them for 1,000 years? That is the position held by premillenialists. The "pre" means that Christ comes to rule before the 1,000 years starts.

Another group believes that John means something different. They say that, for 1,000 years, the gospel will triumph. It is after that that the rule of Christ will begin. Because Christ's rule begins after the 1,000 years, those who believe this interpretation are called post-millenialists.

Others believe that, like so many other elements in Revelation, the number 1,000 is symbolic. Like the numbers ten and one hundred, it stands for completeness or perfection, but now in nearly the most inclusive sense. In that case, the millenium would mean: "the entire time, from the baptism of new believers until their final and complete fellowship with God." That interpretation would not be based on the expectation that a cosmic event might occur. It is, rather, about this time and all times. It means that Christ reigns and saves and fulfills all the time for those who are faithful.

An alternate symbolic interpretation of the number 1,000 is that it is whatever time is necessary for the perfecting of or completing of God's purposes.

The Temporary Binding of Satan (20:1-3)

John's belief in a time when Satan would be bound and Christ would reign on earth for 1,000 years was the further development of other beliefs that the Jews and others had held for many years. But, as he has done with so many other symbols, John has transformed this one to speak to his new understanding of God and of history.

Up to the first century B.C., Jews generally believed that God's messiah would bring God's kingdom to earth, and that the kingdom would last forever on the earth.

Gradually the deepening corruption of the times disillusioned many religious people. The earth, they believed, could not house the eternal perfection of God's kingdom. In place of that belief, they substituted another—God's final kingdom would be in another more acceptable environment.

The millenium is a stage in that thought. It is the belief that, for a while, God will reign on the earth. But eventually, the fullness of God's presence will require a totally new time and place.

The number of years for the kingdom on earth may or may not have been literal for John. It may mean symbolically the time between God's initiating of the kingdom and the completion of it. However the duration is to be understood, the notion of a time of God's rule on the earth fulfills the older expectation for God's kingdom. The end of that time and the new kingdom that follows elsewhere is the new notion.

The battle of Chapter 19 now centers upon the chief antagonist: Satan. All four of his names are used, as though it is he who has appeared in all of these others, but in disguise. As there is one God who finds expression in many ways, so there is one source of evil, dressed in many disguises.

Although Satan is the single evil behind all individual evils, God's angel easily subdues him. The earth is cleansed of Satan for 1,000 years—the time needed to complete God's purpose.

The symbol of the key reminds us that it is God who loosens and binds the powers of life. In the letter to the church at Philadelphia (3:7-13) the *one like a son of man* describes himself as the one *who has the key of David, who opens and no one shall shut, who shuts and no one opens.* Although the angel holds the key now, it is only by permission of God that he does so.

Satan is cast into the bottomless pit. It is not clear why it should be a temporary imprisonment. The pit does not refer to the same place as Hades or Sheol. The earth, for the Jews, was a layer spread out over other layers and habitations and forces. Its depths were the source of earthquakes and other natural phenomena. Its darkness was also forbidding. The exile of Satan, then, is to a realm of dark mystery. References in other parts of the book to brimstone and smoke show that the pit was regarded with fear and seen as a place of torment.

The First Resurrection (20:4-6)

Both Ezekiel and Daniel had spoken of a time when God would gather the faithful and establish a reign upon the earth (Ezekiel 37:15-28; Daniel 7:22, 27). Jews and Christians alike expected the new kingdom to be like the Eden that had been lost to humankind by Adam and Eve.

John redraws that expectation into a time for the earthly reign of the martyrs. By this point in Revelation, the word *martyr* certainly refers to those who had suffered death because of their beliefs. The righteous Christians who die peaceful deaths fall into another category. In verse 4, John indicates that the task of judging was given to those who had been beheaded for their testimony to Jesus. This also helps us understand the possible connection between the *conquerors* and the martyrs as that connection developed in John's understanding. For the first resurrection of the martyrs fulfills the promises made to the conquerors in the letters to the churches. In Chapter 2, verse 11 John records the words, *He who conquers shall not be hurt by the second death.* In 2:26 he reports this promise to the church: *He who conquers and keeps my works to the end, I will give him power over the nations, and he shall rule them with a rod of iron.*

The special role given to the martyrs represents another

refashioning of traditional beliefs under Christian influence. Previously, along with the conviction that God's earthly kingdom would last forever, came the parallel conviction that all of the righteous would be raised from the dead at one time, to enjoy the fruits of the blessed life together. John first divided the kingdom into an earthly one which would last 1,000 years and a heavenly kingdom which would be everlasting. Along with that division comes a further division among those who are raised. For the earthly kingdom, those who were most abused by earthly powers will come to power. For the heavenly kingdom, the rest will enjoy it by virtue of the second resurrection.

The role of the martyrs is both judgmental (verse 4) and priestly (verse 6). From this, many have assumed that the martyrs spend their 1,000 years evangelizing the surrounding nations. That other nations continue to exist during this time can be seen in verse 8. There, John says, after the 1,000 years of his captivity, Satan will again rise to deceive the nations.

Satan's Last Act (20:7-10)

Satan is again loosed. He mobilizes forces against the saints. John's name for the saints' dwelling place, *the Beloved City*, is meant to contrast with the name given by the merchants and kings to Babylon—the great and mighty city.

Gog and *Magog* are spoken of in Ezekiel 38:2. Gog is a ruler; Magog is the land from which he came. They were enemies of God in Old Testament literature, and, for John, symbolize all nations that oppose God's purposes.

Gog and Magog signify a particularly important message. In Ezekiel 38, the Son of man is told to say to Gog that Gog must rise up against Israel. Those uprisings take place at times when the people of Israel think they dwell securely. Three times in that chapter (verses 8, 11, and 14) the message is repeated.

Many of John's readers knew that story. Certainly they understood the reference to Gog as a reference to the perennial source of evil. The story would have been understood by them at two levels.

First, because the actual readers of John's book were the Christians in Asia Minor, they would be warned not to feel overly secure—either in their faith or in their status in the world. In one garb or another, evil might find its easiest access to them when they seem secure and, therefore, less watchful.

Second, within the story John is telling, evil has been bound for a thousand years. Still, it has not been eliminated. It arises from the depths still fueled with the same ambition for domination. No one can doubt the vitality of evil, and should not, until its final demise.

To those two levels of understanding, we can add a third. In John's story, everything appears in contrasts. The height of it all is the contrast of Babylon with the Heavenly City of God. In a sense, Christians live in the midst of those two cities—God's emerging kingdom, evil's receding domain. It is not that one city exists and the other is to come. Rather, the two are at odds with one another throughout history.

Gog represents more than a story from the past. It represents the erratic but predictable upsurge of evil at any time, in any circumstance. Similarly, the *fire from heaven* (verse 9) is not a one-time-only event, but the cauterizing of the world against evil.

The point is that being a Christian is being at the point where those two forces meet and where evil is overcome. In an important way, the story of God and the fire from heaven is an aspect of every Christian's biography.

Like the first battle, this one ends quickly. The devil is cast this time into the brimstone lake and the rest of his retinue is consumed by fire. Under the third interpretation of the millenium, this means that, while the defeat of evil is in God's plans, the time required for its consummation remains a mystery. It will occur at the completion of God's time.

The Death of Death and Hades (20:11-15)

John's attention is turned toward a great throne, so awesome that all of the rest of heaven and earth slip from his sight.

Gradually other persons enter his vision. They are the dead who have been raised again. The record of the lives of each has been kept in God's books. The books are now opened in the presence of each person— each one's life is now an open chapter.

Two kinds of books are mentioned: the records of each person's life and the *book of life* itself. Daniel 7:10 has furnished the idea of the books of judgment. The book of life may have been the one book containing the names of all who had remained faithful.

John again reaffirms his belief that persons are judged by the deeds they do. The books record the actual deeds of persons. His emphasis contrasts somewhat with Paul. Paul believed that no one's deeds would be sufficient for salvation. For him, grace alone would suffice. John holds both themes together in a sometimes difficult tension: People are judged by their deeds, and yet it is not deeds alone, but faithfulness that saves God's people.

Death and Hades yield up their dead, as does the sea. No one is excluded. The belief in a bodily resurrection, implied here in John, forms the basis for some Christian attitudes about burial and cremation; in particular, that we have no right to cremate bodies in the light of God's plan to restore them during the last days. Others view this as a symbolic and dramatic presentation in John—not arguing for a physical resurrection but for his belief that all humans had to make an account of their lives before God.

Even Death and Hades must face judgment. Their suffocating grip on human life comes to an end. They, and those not included in the book of life, face the second death. The second death is that from which no resurrection is possible.

In this scene, the earth is finally scraped clean of its evil. We are led to expect that, in its purified state, it is ready to become the dwelling place of the groom and his bride.

§ § § § § § §

The Message of Revelation 20

In this part, John creates a sequence of scenes that has caused great debate among Christians. That debate has to do with the meaning of the millenium— whether it is literal or symbolic, and whether John thinks that Christ will return to this earth before or after his people reign for 1,000 years.

Amid the debates, there are some common themes. Those themes constitute the message of this part of the book.

§ While evil seems to move freely, it never moves beyond the ability of God to control it.

§ God intends for the faithful to achieve influence among the nations of this world; but that victory is to be the result of God's acts and not of the aggressiveness of God's people. Their task is to remain faithful and to trust God.

§ Ultimately, evil will be overcome.

§ All people must make an account of their lives before God.

§ God's victory will be the death of death itself.

§ § § § § § §

Revelation 21

Introduction to This Chapter

After the worship in heaven and the removal of evil from the earth, one would expect God to constitute either a heavenly or an earthly paradise. John sees it otherwise. Conflict, anger, tears, and violence have filled the calendars of both places. Neither is the proper setting for what God chooses to bring about. God plans a *new heaven and a new earth*.

This, too, has precedent in the Old Testament. Isaiah had written, *Behold, I create new heavens and a new earth, . . .be glad and rejoice forever in that which I create; for behold, I create Jerusalem a rejoicing* (Isaiah 65:17-18).

It is the New Jerusalem, *Jerusalem rejoicing*, that John now portrays. The New Jerusalem is in every way a contrast to Babylon.

Here is an outline of this chapter.

I. A New Heaven and a New Earth (21:1-8)
II. The City of God (21:9-21)
III. The Lamb in the City (21:22-27)
IV. Eden Restored (22:1-5)

This part is laden with symbols, more than we are able to understand. The meanings of certain gems, the significance of the architecture of the city, the design and geography of its setting—each part is densely compacted with meanings. Yet, without knowing them all, we can take in the larger picture. Above all, we are meant to be swept into the grandeur of the New Jerusalem and the brilliance of its ornamentation. Throughout all of the decorative items John has interspersed familiar religious signs and images, so that we can see the New Jerusalem as a fulfillment of all of the ancient dreams about God's glory.

A New Heaven and a New Earth (21:1-8)

John combines two symbols: Jerusalem as the holy dwelling of God and the bride as the one whom God blesses with the divine presence. Neither the old heaven nor the old earth is suitable for the new creation. The new creation outreaches the grasp of either symbol—it is more than a glorified old Jerusalem and more than the simple setting for a wedding. Despite the quantity of its luxury, which John will soon explain, it is the quality of the place that makes it worthy of our attention. It is the place where God chooses to dwell. It is the place of God's personal care for the faithful. It is the place where tears and mourning have vanished and death is no more.

In verse 5, John's pastoral concerns come to the forefront. He draws from what he sees in his vision a message for the people to whom he is writing. As always throughout his book, he has his eyes upon the vision, but his mind and heart rest with the burdened Christians of first-century Asia Minor. The meaning of his vision, translated for those Christians, is found in verses 6-7: *To the thirsty I will give from the fountain of the water of life without payment. He who conquers shall have this heritage, and I will be his God and he shall be my son.* He follows this rich promise with a warning to the cowardly, faithless, polluted, fornicators, and others that they shall not escape the second death. The moral point of the vision of the new heaven and earth is the same point that John has made throughout the book: Be faithful; God is just and true.

The City of God (21:9-21)

Chapter 17 began with one of the seven angels of the bowls saying, *Come, I will show you the judgment of the great harlot*. John continues his use of contrasts in Revelation 21:9 with an angel of the bowls now inviting him to *Come, I will show you the Bride, the wife of the Lamb.* The bride shown to John is not a woman, but a city. The city, of course, is John's most elaborate symbol. Imagine the people of faith as a city. What would it be like? For one thing, it would not be like the harlot.

To further the contrast, he is taken to the mountains to view the bride, the holy city, as Moses had been taken to the mountaintop to view the holy commandments. It was to the desert that the angel had taken John to view Babylon.

The name *Jerusalem* for the new city shows the continuity between the hopes of the Jews and those of the early Christians. Although, in many cities of Asia Minor, Jews and Christians resented and at times conspired against one another, the early Church had no doubt that the faith of the Jewish tradition prepared the basis for its own.

The description of the holy city demonstrates the same interest in continuity. The city has twelve gates with twelve angels (twelve is a sacred number to the Jews). The city's gates bear the names of Israel's twelve tribes. On the foundations are the names of the twelve disciples. Each has its place on one and the same structure. Much that John includes had been described already in Ezekiel 42:16-19. John has made a profound Christian use of a traditional Jewish book. The holy city, the bride, is made up of the people of faith from throughout the history of the Jews and Christians.

The city he describes is enormous and bejeweled. The angel measures it for John. *Twelve thousand stadia* equal about 1,500 miles. The stones and jewels decorating the wall are those that Jews would recognize from passages in the Old Testament about the decoration of the high priest's breastplate (see Exodus 28:17-20.) Isaiah 54:11-12 mentions them as well.

Deep within many Eastern religions are vestiges of other religions that were absorbed by one another throughout time. Nothing was absorbed intact, however. The Jews did with other religions what the Christians did with that of the Jews: took in and converted their symbols to make them serve another purpose. For Christians it was also a matter of demonstrating that, eventually, everything shall be made to serve and worship the one God. The jewels that adorned the New Jerusalem and the Jewish high priest's breastplate are a case in point. They come from the signs of the zodiac in astrology.

Astrology was an ancient fascination. Religious people had for years searched the stars for clues about the nature of the universe and the will of God. Many constellations had been plotted, given religious significance, and tied in with creatures and jewels used in worship. Here is a list of the heavenly constellations and the jewels that symbolize them. Both were a feature of ancient religions of the Near East.

CREATURES	JEWELS
ram	amethyst
bull	hyacinth
twins	chrysoprase
crab	topaz
lion	beryl
virgin	chrysolite
balance	sardius
scorpion	sardonyx
archer	smaragdus (emerald)
goat	chalcedon
water carriers	sapphire
fish	jasper

That list of creatures comprises the signs of the zodiac. They represent the order in which the sun travels through the constellations. Interestingly, John reverses their order, as though to say that Christ can witness through anything, but he turns it in his own way. If the city is the bride, then, within its people are those who have found how to make the religions of the earth make their witness to the one true God.

The symbolism overpowers literal meaning. Words are inadequate to say what John wants to say (remember he not only tells us what he sees, but he has to search his own vocabulary to describe and interpret it). He asks us to imagine things that defy our experience, partly to show that what he describes lies outside our experience, even outside our limited language to describe. He speaks of gold that is transparent and of gates made from a single pearl. He searches for ways to show that God's kingdom beggars anyone's ability to grasp it. Nonetheless, we can understand enough to know that it is a fulfillment of what we have been promised, and not a total rejection of it. That is the reason for the connection to the twelve tribes and twelve disciples. Whatever it is, it fulfills the promises of God and Christ.

The Lamb in the City (21:22-27)

John changes imagery. The new city has no temple. The temple was a symbol of something that Jews and Christians alike hungered for: God's presence. Now God's presence itself will be the temple. God's presence fills the city. God is the light of those who dwell there; the lamb is their lamp. Appropriately, it is Christ who supports the light, but God alone is the true light. This fulfilled one of the brightest of Isaiah's prophecies:

> Arise, shine; for your light has come,
>   and the glory of the Lord has risen upon you.
> The sun shall be no more your light by day,
>   nor for brightness shall the moon give light
>   to you by night,

but the Lord will be your everlasting light,
   and your God will be your glory.

(Isaiah 60:1, 19)

The same chapter of Isaiah also speaks of open gates, and of the kings and wealth of nations passing through them.
John recites the same belief in verses 24-26 as he tells the details of the holy city:

By its light shall the nations walk; and the kings of the earth shall bring their glory into it, and its gates shall never be shut by day—and there shall be no night there; they shall bring into it the glory and the honor of the nations.

John then reminds his readers of another aspect of that city. Its gates shall close to some—to the unclean, the liars, the abominators, and those not in the Lamb's book of life. Clearly, as he enlarges his picture of God's glory he increases the warnings to the Christians to remain pure. They would understand.

Eden Restored (22:1-5)

As John moves closer to the heart of the heavenly city, he harvests more and more of his rich symbolic tradition, seeking words and images to evoke in others the awe and wonder he feels; seeking also, each step of the way, to bring them to the intensity of faith that he feels.
As the Book of Genesis explains human alienation by telling the story of Adam and Eve's expulsion from the idyllic garden of Eden, so John portrays the new paradise with elements of that garden. The tree of life and the water of life come from the story of Eden (Genesis 2:9), although this new garden goes far beyond the original. Ezekiel had also spoken of new living waters, flowing from God's restored land (47:6-12). From the Psalms comes the promise to see God's face (17:15). Leaves of healing appear first in Ezekiel (47:12). The end of night

136   REVELATION

and darkness is a hope first registered by the prophet Zechariah (14:7).

The promise that God's name shall be on the foreheads of God's people brings out a remarkable broadening of an Old Testament idea. In Exodus 28:36-38, the high priests alone were allowed to have God's name upon their foreheads. Now all have that name; now, in God's kingdom, all are priests.

Names on the forehead also served as signs of ownership. In previous chapters we have seen how the beast and God both inscribed their names on the foreheads of the faithful. Slaves also could bear the names of their master. Combined, these two sets of symbols present a basic tenet of Christian theology: those who belong to God become priests to one another.

§ § § § § § §

The Message of Revelation 21

This part opens before our eyes the grandeur of God's plans for the church. For this to come to pass, however, everything must be made new—heaven and earth. Not that all from the past fades into eternal forgetfulness. It does not. Instead, John collects the bright images of hope from the Old Testament and uses them to explain this new thing God has done. He also shows how, when God uses them, those things become something more and greater than anyone expected.

From the greatest to the smallest, John shows God's acts. The enormous city is created, and yet every small tear is wiped from the martyr's eye. From the heights of the mountain John sees the new city, yet from the memory of the story of the garden of Eden he is able to understand its significance. From the magnificance of its decoration he can sense the elegance of the city, yet, from the meekness of the Lamb he senses that God is the city's true light.

From these contrasts John derives the message of this chapter. We must always be aware that each thing he presents in his book had a moral to be drawn for his first century readers, and for us.

§ Although we may be overwhelmed with awe at God, God is tender, and knows and cares for our individual pains and grief.

§ The symbols we have known and used to understand God and God's kingdom are all essential, but what God offers us goes far beyond them. They are hints, not photographs.

§ God's heavenly kingdom is a place where God dwells in the midst of God's people.

§ Christ is the bearer of God's light.

§ § § § § § §

Revelation 22

Introduction to This Chapter

In this part, John presents the final words of the angel of the bowl and of Jesus. He also speaks again to point out the moral and message of all that he has told his readers. The epilogue (*epilogue* means *final word*) interprets the practical meaning of Jesus' revelation, to make certain no reader misunderstands what is at stake.

The epilogue has the following parts:

I. The Testimony of Christ (22:6-7)
II. The Testimony of John (22:8-9)
III. The Testimony of the Angel (22:10-11)
IV. The Full Nature of Christ (22:12-16)
V. A Last Invitation and Warning (22:17-19)
VI. A Final Promise and Blessing (22:20-21)

In this last part, John picks up several themes and motifs from the previous chapters. He assumes that his readers have read from beginning to end, and that they will need only to have certain symbols elevated for a moment for their significance to be recalled. So his readers are once more exhorted to keep the words of the prophecy. Again, John tries to worship an angel and is rebuffed. Again comes the warning that the time of the end is near. The symbols of *Alpha and Omega*, of *washed robes*, and of *gates* appear. Warnings are given to fornicators and idolators again. And the *root of David* is recalled as a metaphor for Jesus. One more time we hear of the bride of Christ, of the call to drink the water of life, of the plagues, and of the tree of life.

Clearly, John intends this as the summary of his sermon as well as a moral exhortation to keep the faith.

The Testimony of Christ (22:6-7)

The angel has been speaking on behalf of God. The same God has, through the Spirit, spoken through the spirits of the prophets. Now the angel speaks as though it were quoting the very words of Christ: *Behold, I am coming soon.*

John assures his readers that it was God who inspired the prophets. That reinforces his own use of the prophetic books throughout Revelation. It also allows him to reinforce the claims he makes on behalf of his own book. John is a prophet. The same spirit that inspired Isaiah and Daniel inspires him.

That reminder about inspiration is enough to certify the integrity of his book. On that basis, then, he also can promise a blessing to those who keep the words of its prophecies. The verb *keep* here means more than to place something on the shelf. It has something to do with *safe keeping*, but also to do with keeping the words in mind and adapting one's behaviors to them.

The Testimony of John (22:8-9)

John vouches for the truth of his report. As in 19:10, he seeks to worship the angel who is leading him and who brought him God's words. However, it may be here that he is simply retelling the earlier experience in order to remind his readers who he is and to re-emphasize the message. In either case, the angel's response carries the point: No creature is to worship another creature. If even the angels in heaven are not to be worshiped, how much less ought one to worship emperors or marble gods in granite shrines.

John may have chosen to repeat this incident with the angel for another reason. Angels play a very prominent role in Revelation. It would be easy for his readers to fall into a pattern of worshiping angels, at least of viewing them as important go-betweens to gain access to God. There is evidence of angel worship in the Jewish tradition—especially in books that were widely used among the Jews but which did not become a part of the Protestant Bible. Other similar books contain strong warnings against praying to angels—which lets us know that something of that sort was going on and was widespread enough that warnings were needed.

Angel worship continued into some pockets of the Christian tradition. Paul warns against it in Colossians 2:18. Warnings appear in other places as well. John made his point clear: Angels are God's messengers, but they are not to be worshiped.

John adjusts the angel's words, now, to make certain that they do two things: (1) identify John as one of the prophets; (2) identify his book as a prophetic book. The angel's words also underscore the earlier message of the equality of all who keep the words of the book.

Keeping the words does not mean to copy out the exact words or not to change the exact wording of the book. John tells and retells stories and events in several ways in the book, as we have seen. To *keep the words* does not mean to keep the words as they are, but to keep their meanings (his message). It means to safeguard the message and adapt one's behavior to it.

The angel tells John, immediately following the order to keep the words, to *worship God*. The point of the prophecies, then, is not to put a set of words at the center of worship, but to allow the words to point to God. God alone is worthy of worship.

The Testimony of the Angel (22:10-11)

The angel also speaks of the nearness of the time when the prophecies will be fulfilled. The message is meant not just for John, but for John's first-century readers. They need to take the warnings to heart.

The words of the prophecy are not to be sealed up. Many of the older apocalyptic books had been given along with an order to seal them up until the time was ripe. For example, Daniel says that he was ordered to seal up his prophecies. John's book, however was not about some distant future. It was about the time soon to come.

The angel says to let the evildoers still do evil and the righteous still do right. That is not an order to let things be. It is a form of warning: Let those who insist on doing evil continue to do so; they will soon see the full meaning of what they do. And, above all, let the righteous continue to do right, for they shall be blessed when they see the full meaning of what they do.

The Full Nature of Christ (22:12-16)

The quotation marks in this paragraph are confusing. It is Christ, not the angel, who speaks. Christ promises to come and to *recompense* all for what they have done. In Greek, the phrase means *to give due wages* for what has been done. The work for which one is paid is the faithful and moral life. Behavior matters; it matters ultimately!

The Christ who comes is the alpha and the omega (the first and the last, the beginning and the end). Those words had been applied to God in Revelation 1:12. Now, applied to Christ, they bear great meaning. God is in Christ; in God, Christ is also the beginning and the end.

John next addresses his readers, to make certain that his readers apply the meaning of what they have just read to their churches. *Those who wash their robes* is shorthand for those who have been cleansed by the Lamb's blood.

In the seven churches of Asia Minor, all of the old temptations continued to dog the faithful. Only the faithful know that the fornicator and the idolator are allies of the beast; and only they know that a new kingdom is pressing in after the old.

The speaker in verse 16 is again Jesus. He identifies himself with the root of David, showing the important connection between the witnesses of the Jewish and Christian traditions. Jesus authenticates John's message, saying that he has seen the angel with the message. This also identifies Jesus with the God from whom all of the promises to Israel have come.

A Last Invitation and Warning (22:17-19)

The church in the vision (the Spirit and the bride) now speaks to the church on earth. The heavenly church bids the faithful to come. In heaven there is the water of life; those who thirst for the true God may come to drink without limit.

John also issues a warning to all who hear the words of the prophecy in his book—no one is to add to or take away from the words of the prophecy. The promises of the book will be withdrawn from those who mar its pages. They will not have access to the tree of life—another reference to the garden of Eden.

John was not the first, nor was he the last, to place a warning in his book to those who might add or subtract from what he has written. Moses gives a similar warning in Deuteronomy 4:2. Other apocalyptic books which are not in the Bible warn the reader to change nothing in their texts. Even early Christian teachers and Jewish rabbis have written notes accompanying their books, to prevent anyone from tampering with the texts. Some of them included threats similar to John's. This is not a threat that all must interpret the book literally. John has knowingly used symbols from several sources. He has also acknowledged that he did not record everything he saw.

But during John's time, several Christian documents had begun to appear with which copyists or writers had taken great liberties. Several "gospels" would appear before long, as well, each one more fantastic than the last. As this process went on, the image and message of Jesus became increasingly magical. John was on Patmos, a prisoner because of his witness to Jesus. He did not want that witness compromised. So, borrowing from the story of the garden of Eden, he warns those who misuse his message that they will suffer the fate of Adam; they will be barred from access to the tree of life.

A Final Promise and Blessing (22:20-21)
John now quotes the words of Jesus. The promise has echoes throughout the book: *Surely I am coming soon.*

John's response is the familiar, *Amen. Come, Lord Jesus.* That phrase is often spoken by Christians in its original biblical form: *Maranatha.*

The final verse uses a word that appears rarely in the Book of Revelation. That word is *grace.* In this case, John does not use the word with the heavy theological meaning that Paul does. This is not a doctrine of salvation by grace alone. It is much more in the Old Testament mode, and means *God's gracious presence.*

From the perspective of the end of John's book, we can see more clearly how the parts fit together. In the background, behind all of the events, stories, and parables, there is one grand story. That story is the dramatic comparison between the heavenly city and the earthly city.

The church on earth is engaged in a heroic journey from one city to the other. Like the knights in medieval epics, the people must keep true to their vows. But the journey is fraught with dangers. The greatest danger is that the church itself will become confused, and will take the earthly city to be the heavenly city, or, from lack of evidence, lose its belief that there is a heavenly city.

The letters to the churches assure their members that God is watching them, is aware of them, and wants them to complete their journey of faith. In each event that follows, John cuts away larger and larger portions of the glitter of the earthly city, revealing two things in the process: the evil that lies at its heart, and the magnificence of God who promises the heavenly city.

In the midst of each stage, John stops for an interlude. Christians are shown worshiping the true God. Heaven's hearth is laid open for the church to see. In those brief vignettes, John reminds Christians that the true journey is to worship and remain faithful. He also shows them that those who have died in their cause have already found their home in the Lord.

To help his readers grasp the magnitude of what is at stake, John makes the stage for his story larger with each scene. First it is the seven cities of Asia Minor. Then it increases its range in both the heavens and the earth until it becomes the cosmic struggle between the source of all evil and the source of all good. The church must continue its faithful journey, while, at each stage, it sees that the dimensions of the strife that surrounds and engages it enlarge.

When John reaches the conclusion of his story of stories, he has left no doubt of the outcome. He then focuses his attention back on the church on earth. He mixes promises of blessing with words of warning; and always he reiterates that the story he has told, and the victory he has described, will come true soon. He wants his readers to know that, always, there lies just by the horizon the imminent heavenly city of God.

§ § § § § § §

The Message of Revelation 22

In this chapter, John tells his readers how they are to take his book. He also, once more, lets them know what is at stake in the strife they are experiencing. He therefore condenses the message of the entire book into several brief segments, each one holding up a portion of the message he wants all to remember. The message is:

§ His readers must live and act in the knowledge that God's kingdom is coming soon.

§ John is a prophet, and stands as an equal to all of the other prophets of the Jewish and Christian tradition.

§ His words must not be altered, but kept—that is, they must be acted upon.

§ The one who gives John his message is Christ.

§ God is in Christ, and Christ can be identified with God as the alpha and omega, the first and the last.

§ The holy city is like the garden of Eden, containing the water of life.

§ The gracious presence of Christ will be with the saints, that is, those who believe and trust in his word.

§ § § § § § §

Glossary of Terms

Abaddon: Hebrew word meaning the land of darkness and death; John treats it as the personal name of the destroyer of life and hope.

Acropolis: A fortress that was well placed in order to defend cities.

Alpha and Omega: The first and the last, or the beginning and the end; from the first (*alpha*) and the last (*omega*) letters of the Greek alphabet.

Amethyst: A purple, transparent quartz crystal.

Amulet: An object carried by a person usually as a charm against illness or other harm.

Angel: A messenger, especially a messenger from God; often a special category of heavenly being.

Antiochus: Ruler of Syria who persecuted the Jews and who placed a statue of Zeus on the altar of the Temple in Jerusalem in 168 B.C.

Apocalypse: The Greek word that is translated *revelation*. It means literally *to remove the veil*, or to reveal what has been hidden. The Book of Revelation is sometimes called The Apocalypse (of John).

Apollyon: A probable reference to the Greek god Apollo, the god of the sun and of prophecy, to whom several Roman emperors were devoted.

Ark of the covenant: A chest containing the two stone tablets bearing the Ten Commandments. It was kept in the holiest part of the ancient Jewish tabernacle, the Holy of Holies (see Exodus 25:10).

Artemis: Goddess of the hunt and of the moon. Apollo's sister. Many cities, including Ephesus, had temples to Artemis. Her temple in Ephesus was one of the seven wonders of the ancient world.

Balaam: A prophet hired by Balak to curse the Israelites; when Balaam beat his donkey, it reprimanded him (see Numbers 22–24). Balaam is also accused of trying to get Israel to follow immoral practices (Numbers 31:16).

Beryl: A sea-green gem.

Carnelian: Red quartz, used for jewelry.

Chalcedony: Quartz, usually gray or milky in color, with a lustrous surface.

Chrysolite: A yellow topaz.

Chrysoprase: Quartz, apple green in color; a gemstone.

Denarius: A Roman silver coin, equivalent, in John's time, to about one day's wages.

Desecration: The period when Antiochus placed a statue of Zeus on the altar of the Temple in Jerusalem. It became a symbolic word, referring to any spoiling of a holy place.

Endurance: A special word in the Book of Revelation, meaning to wait for Jesus steadfastly, through suffering and persecution.

Ephesus: A very prosperous ancient city in Asia Minor, located near the Aegean Sea. It was the site of the temple of Artemis.

Epilogue: Words spoken at the conclusion. Usually a short speech or comment in summary.

Euphrates: The largest river located in western Asia. It separated the farthest reach of the Roman Empire from the region of Parthia.

Hades: In Hebrew, the realm of the dead (also called Sheol); sometimes, as in Revelation 20:13-14, the realm only of the wicked.

Hanukkah: A feast celebrated by the Jews in remembrance of the time they regained their Temple in Jerusalem after Antiochus had desecrated it by placing a statue of Zeus on its altar.

Hyacinth: A red or cinnamon-colored gemstone that was transparent.

Jasper: Possibly the same in Revelation as the modern jasper stone, which is quartz of a red, brown, or yellow color. It may also have been a valuable green jade.

Koine: A dialect of Greek. The language of ordinary conversation.

Laodicea: A city of Asia Minor, famous as a center for banking, commerce, and the manufacture of clothes and carpets of native black wool.

Martyr: A witness; one who tells about the nature and significance of Christ. Martyrs gradually came to be identified with those who died because of their faith in Christ.

Menorah: A seven-branched candle holder, used in the Jewish Temple, and symbolizing the seven days of Creation. Exodus 25:31-40 and 37:17-24 describe the appearance of the menorah.

Millenium: A time span of one thousand years. A time when the faithful will rule on the earth. It may also refer, symbolically, to the time necessary for God's kingdom to come to completion.

Mystery: Something not knowable by human means.

Nebuchadnezzar: Also called Nebuchadrezzar. King of Babylon from 605-562 B.C. He destroyed Jerusalem and carried the Jews into captivity.

Nicolaitans: Possibly the Greek translation for the word *Balaam*. It means literally *followers of Nicholas*. It may refer to those who taught that, once saved, Christians were free to do immoral acts without fear of sin.

Nimbus: Originally a bright cloud that supposedly accompanied the appearance of gods and goddesses. In Christian tradition, a halo or shiny disk over the heads of saints and angels.

Papyrus: Sheets from an Egyptian plant, dried and placed end to end. Papyrus was placed on a scroll and used for writing.

Parthia, Parthians: An ancient country in Western Asia, near modern northeast Iran. Parthian soldiers were famous archers who were greatly feared by the Romans near the Euphrates River.

Patmos: A small prison island located in the region west of Asia Minor.

Pergamum: A city of Asia Minor, famous for its medical center. Also the center of the imperial cult in Asia Minor.

Pestilence: A fatal epidemic or plague.

Philadelphia: A city of ancient Asia Minor, a gateway to the East. It was known for its fine grapes, hot springs, and its worship of Dionysus and other gods.

Portent: A sign or wonder. Usually one carrying a special meaning or message. In Revelation, a portent carries a message about the meaning of history, especially the future.

Prologue: An introduction to a book or play. Its length is usually brief.

Proconsul: Governor of a Roman province.

Prophecy: (noun) An inspired utterance of a prophet; usually declaring the divine will.

Prophesy: (verb) Literally, to speak beforehand; to reveal the message of God. In Revelation, it means also to declare the secrets of God.

Prophet: One who speaks beforehand. One who speaks on God's behalf. New Testament prophets are those who tell about Jesus and his witness to God.

Revelation: Literally, to remove the veil. In the New Testament it means God's self-giving to people as well as the unveiling of certain facts.

Sapphire: A blue, transparent gemstone.

Sardis: A Roman city in central Asia Minor. A wealthy commercial center, also a popular location for the worship of various gods of nature.

Sardius: A stone; a form of chalcedony, usually deep orange in color.

Sardonyx: A kind of chalcedony, with white and brown bands.

Satan: At first, a prosecutor on God's behalf; hence, an accuser. In Revelation, Satan is the one who tempts people away from God; therefore, the principal force in opposition to God.

Shekinah: The manifestation of God, or the presence of God, in Jewish tought.

Smaragdus: A gemstone, light green in color. Possibly an emerald.

Smyrna: A coastal city of Asia Minor, known for its wealth and its natural beauty. It was one of the first cities to engage in worship of the Roman emperor.

Spirit: As Spirit (capital "S"), the active presence of God. As spirit (small "s") in phrases like *the seven spirits*, it refers to the fullness of God's presence. The Spirit does God's work and inspires prophecy.

Synagogue: A Jewish local congregation. Places for Jews to teach and worship after they were expelled from Jerusalem by the Babylonians.

Tent of Meeting: The shelter for the ark of the covenant, where God was revealed to Moses.

Thyatira: An inland city located in Asia Minor and an important trading center. It had a great many trade and craft guilds.

Topaz: A gemstone, usually brown or pink.

Tribulation: A time of serious affliction. Taken from the word describing the place where grain was threshed.

Typology: A form of writing that makes the pattern of one event look like the pattern of another event. In the Book of Revelation, John patterns many events after those that occurred in the Exodus.

Witness: One who sees and can tell what has been seen, especially one who has seen an important truth. *Witness* can be a verb (*to witness*) and refer to the act of telling. It can also be a noun, from which it has two meanings: (1) the person who has seen; (2) the thing that has been seen. In the latter sense, the witness of the martyrs is what they have seen in Jesus; the witness of Jesus is what Jesus has seen and said of God.

Wormwood: A plant yielding a bitter abstract, used in making absinth. It has a harsh and bitter taste.

Yom Kippur: A Jewish holy day. A time of penitence. It was celebrated by sacrificing animals and by symbolically affixing the sins of the people to two animals, one of which was then driven into the wilderness, the other of which was sacrificed at the altar.

Guide to Pronunciation

Abaddon: Ah-BAD-don
Acropolis: Ah-CRAH-poh-liss
Alpha: AL-fah
Amethyst: AM-eh-thist
Amulet: AM-you-let
Antiochus: An-TIE-oh-kuss
Apocalypse: Ah-POCK-ah-lips
Apocalyptic: Ah-pock-ah-LIP-tik
Apollo: Ah-PAHL-oh
Apollyon: Ah-PAHL-yon
Artemis: AHR-teh-miss
Augustus: Ah-GUSS-tuss
Balaam: BAY-lum
Beryl: BEHR-ill
Caligula: Kah-LIG-you-lah
Carnelian: Kar-NEEL-yen
Chalcedony: Kal-SEH-doh-nee
Chrysolite: KRIS-oh-light
Chrysoprase: KRIS-oh-prays
Claudius: CLAH-dee-us
Denarius: Deh-NAIR-ee-us
Desecration: Deh-seh-KRAY-shun
Domitian: Doh-MIH-shun
Ephesus: EH-fuh-sus
Epilogue: EH-pih-log
Euphrates: You-FRAY-teez

Hades: HAY-deez
Hanukkah: HAH-nah-kuh
Hyacinth: HIGH-ah-sinth
Jezebel: JEH-zeh-bell
Koine: Koy-NAY
Laodicea: Lay-oh-dih-SEE-ah
Martyr: MAHR-ter
Messiah: Meh-SIGH-ah
Menorah: Meh-NOR-ah
Millenium: Mih-LEH-nee-um
Nebuchadrezzar: Neh-buh-keh-DREH-zar
Nicolaitans: Nih-koh-LAY-tons
Nimbus: NIM-bus
Papyrus: Pah-PIE-russ
Parthia: PAHR-thee-ah
Patmos: PAT-moss
Pergamum: Per-GAH-mum
Pestilence: PEST-eh-lents
Portent: POR-tent
Proconsul: Pro-KON-sul
Prologue: PRO-log
Prophecy: PRAH-feh-see
Prophesy: PRAH-feh-sigh
Sapphire: SAFF-ire
Sardis: SAHR-dis
Sardonyx: Sar-DAH-niks
Shekinah: Sheh-KIGH-nah
Smaragdus: Smeh-RAG-dus
Smyrna: SMER-nah
Synagogue: SIN-ah-gog
Thyatira: Thee-ah-TEE-rah
Tiberius: Tie-BEER-ee-us
Topaz: TOH-paz
Tribulation: Trib-you-LAY-shun
Typology: Tie-PAH-leh-jee
Vitellius: Vih-TELL-ee-us
Yom Kippur: Yom-Kih-POOR

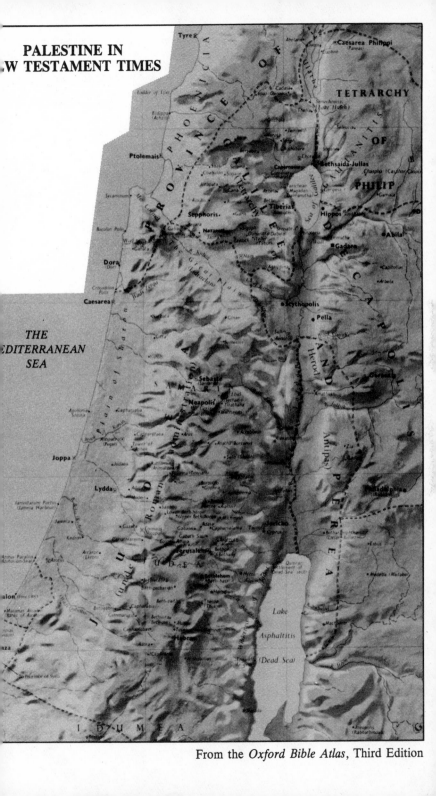

PALESTINE IN
W TESTAMENT TIMES

Tyre

PHOENICIA

TETRARCHY

OF

PHILIP

Ptolemais

Sepphoris

Nazareth

Tiberias

Sea of Galilee

Hippos

Abila

Dora

Gadara

Caesarea

Scythopolis

Pella

THE
MEDITERRANEAN
SEA

Sebaste

Neapolis

Joppa

Lydda

Philadelphia

Jerusalem

JUDAEA

Bethlehem

Lake
Asphaltitis
(Dead Sea)

IDUMEA

From the *Oxford Bible Atlas*, Third Edition

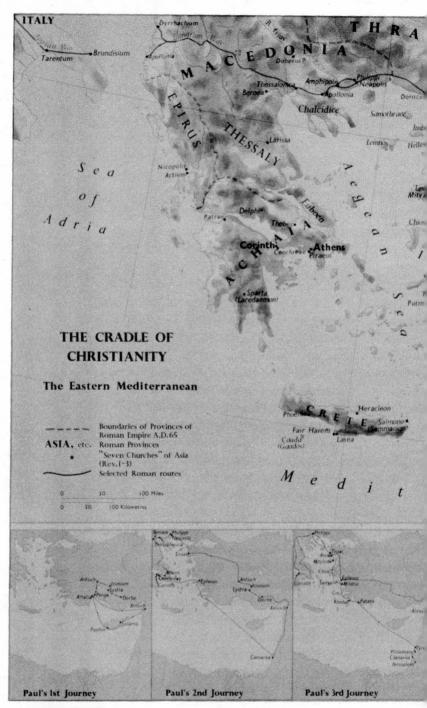

ITALY

Tarentum • *Brundisium*

Ionian Sea

Dyrrhachium

Apollonia

MACEDONIA

Doberus?

THRA

Thessalonica
Beroea •

Amphipolis
Apollonia

Philippi
Neapolis

Doriscu

Chalcidice

Samothrace

EPIRUS

THESSALY

Larissa

AEGEAN

Lemnos

Imb

Hello

Nicopolis
Actium

Sea

Euboea

Les
Mity

of

Delphi

Chio

Patrae

Thebes

Adria

ACHAIA

Corinth

Cenchreae

Athens
Piraeus

Patm

Sparta
(Lacedaemon)

Aegean Sea

THE CRADLE OF CHRISTIANITY

The Eastern Mediterranean

CRETE

Heracleon

Phoenix

Salmone
(Sammonium)

Fair Havens

Canda
(Gaudos)

Lasea

ASIA, etc.
★

Boundaries of Provinces of
Roman Empire A.D. 65
Roman Provinces
"Seven Churches" of Asia
(Rev. 1–3)
Selected Roman routes

Medit

0   50   100 Miles
0   50   100 Kilometres

Paul's 1st Journey

Antioch
Iconium
Lystra
Derbe
Attalia *Perga*
Antioch
Paphos
Salamis

Paul's 2nd Journey

Beroea *Philippi*
Neapolis
Thessalonica
Troas
Athens *Assos*
Mitylene
Corinth
Ephesus
Antioch
Lystra
Iconium
Derbe
Antioch
Caesarea

Paul's 3rd Journey

Philippi
Troas
Assos
Mitylene
Chios
Corinth *Samos*
Ephesus
Miletus
Cos
Rhodes *Patara*
Ptolemais
Caesarea
Jerusalem
Tyre

ASIA MINOR

From the *Oxford Bible Atlas*, Third Edition